HOTEL ORGANIZATIONAL STRUCTURE

DMITRY KOZLOV

About the author

Author of this textbook is Dmitry Kozlov – Ph.D., associate professor of the department of Hospitality, tourism and sports of Plekhanov Russian University of Economics, Moscow, Russian Federation.

The textbook covers the fundamentals of organizational structure of hotels: from the basics of organizational design to the detailed structures of common hotel departments.

Kozlov D.A.

Hotel organizational structure. USA. CreateSpace, 2018.

The book is intended for bachelor and master's programs, studying hotel business and also for specialists in the field of hotel business.

ISBN: 1984122223
ISBN-13: 978-1984122223

TABLE OF CONTENTS

INTRODUCTION

Modern hotels are very complex. Regardless of type or size, any hotel needs an organizational structure. Organizational structure is used to carry out of every daily operations, to divide working tasks between hotel staff, clearly define all the functions for each hotel department, and delegate authority. Proper organizational structure helps to increase efficiency and productivity and overall performance of hotel.

This textbook is dedicated to base issues of hotel organizational structure.

In the first chapter the types of organizational structures is considered. The organizational structure is depended on hotel size. So, it is necessary to know what type of structure is the most appropriate to specific hotel. Besides, type of organizational structure may depend on specific goals of enterprise at specific moment in time.

Second chapter is dedicated to organizational design. Any organization passes there stages of its development. Managers should know on what stage they are and what to do to change their current stage.

Third chapter is the biggest. It addresses issues regarding organizational structures of almost all known hotel departments. Of course, not all positions are represented in all hotels. But in this textbook almost all possibilities are described.

This textbook is intended for bachelor and master's programs, studying hotel business and also for any specialists in hotel business.

Chapter 1. Types of organizational structures in hotels

Organizational structure is a set of organizational units and their interrelations, within the framework of which administrative tasks are distributed among divisions, powers and responsibility of managers and officials are determined.

The organizational structure, on the one hand, is built in accordance with the tasks that the organization poses its strategy. On the other hand, the structure at different levels ensures the use of economies of scale to save the resources of the organization. Thus, the structure links external strategic efficiency with internal efficiency.

The distribution of tasks between departments and managers, the distribution of powers and responsibilities should remain stable for some time to ensure the reproduction and maintenance of the strategy.

In those cases when the strategy changes, or when the structure is recognized as ineffective, reorganization takes place. Reorganization can have both a global character and change the principle of building a structure, and solve local problems of individual units and their relationships. Any reorganization should help to improve the orderliness and effectiveness of the structure.

At the same time, the structure is constantly subjected to a kind of degradation, which simplifies and dilutes the distribution of tasks, powers and responsibilities. Thus, in parallel with the process of organizing and improving efficiency in the structure, the process of disorganization and destruction takes place. Therefore, any formal organizational structure is always different from the actual structure.

Types of organizational structures:
1. «Bureaucratic»:
  – linear
  – linear-staff
  – functional
  – linear-functional
  – divisional:
    – divisional-functional
    – divisional-product
    – divisional-consumer
    – global divisional (with international branches)

2. «Adaptive»:
- project
- matrix (mixed)
- integration
- free.

Table 1.

Features of bureaucratic and adaptive structures

Bureaucratic structures	Adaptive structures
They have proved themselves in stable, unchanging conditions	More suitable for work in unstable conditions, when problems and necessary actions can not be decomposed into elements and distributed specifically between specialists
The problems and tasks faced by the organization are divided into many small ones that are entrusted to individual departments, specialists	Personnel must solve their own problems based on the objectives of the company as a whole. A significant part of their duties are constantly being reviewed due to changing conditions
Each division solves its task separately from the tasks of the organization as a whole	Personnel interact both vertically and horizontally, the system does not prohibit acting by leaping over the steps of the office ladder
The rights and duties of each specialist are detailed, rigidly defined and do not change	Encourages initiatives, creativity
Only top management decides how much the individual tasks performed by the units are consistent with the goals of the organization	
Relations between units located on the same level of the organizational structure are carried out by senior management	
Enforcement is encouraged	

Bureaucratic types

Linear organizational structure

It is characterized by a vertical: the highest leader – the line manager (unit) – the executors. There have only vertical connections. In simple organizations, there are no separate functional units. This structure is built without the allocation of functions.

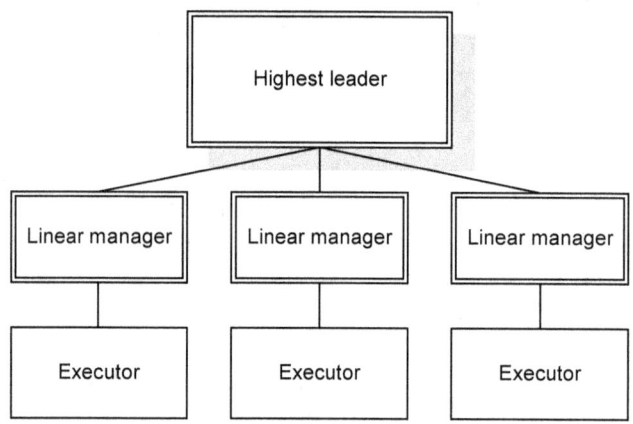

Figure 1. Linear organizational structure

Advantages: simplicity, specificity of tasks and implementers; unity and clarity of management; personal subordination of the performer to one person; full responsibility of the manager for the performance of subordinate units; efficiency in decision-making; coordinated actions of performers.

Disadvantages: high requirements for the qualifications of managers and a high manager's load. The linear structure is applied and effective in small enterprises with simple technology and minimal specialization; increased time of information flow; overloading of top-level managers (a huge amount of information, a stream of papers, many contacts with subordinates and superiors).

Linear-Staff Organizational Structure

As the enterprise grows, as a rule, the linear structure is transformed into a linear-staff structure. It is similar to the previous one, but the management is concentrated in the «headquarters». A group of personnel appears who do not directly give orders to performers, but they carry out consulting work and prepare management decisions.

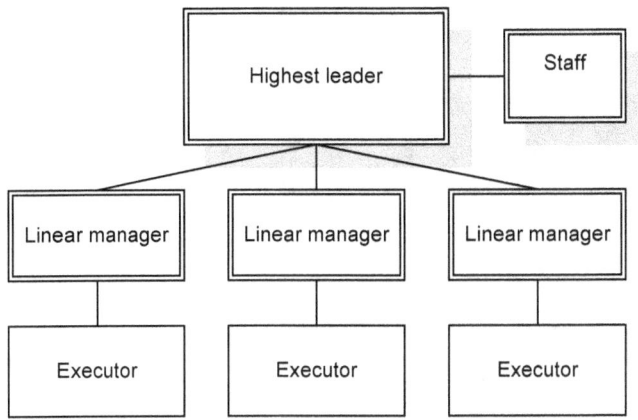

Figure 2. Linear-staff organizational structure

Advantages: a deeper and more meaningful preparation of managerial decisions; release of linear managers from excessive load; the possibility of attracting specialists in certain areas.

Disadvantages: lack of clear responsibility; the preparing decision does not participate in its implementation; the tendency towards excessive centralization; maintaining high requirements for top management making decisions; lag of information.

Functional organizational structure

With further complication of production, the need arises for the specialization of workers, sections, departments, etc., a functional management structure is formed. The distribution of work is according to functions.

With a functional structure, the organization is divided into elements, each of which has a specific function, tasks. It is typical for organizations with a small nomenclature, stability of external conditions. Here there is a vertical: the head – the functional managers (production, marketing, finance) – executors. There are vertical and inter-level links. The functions of the manager are blurred.

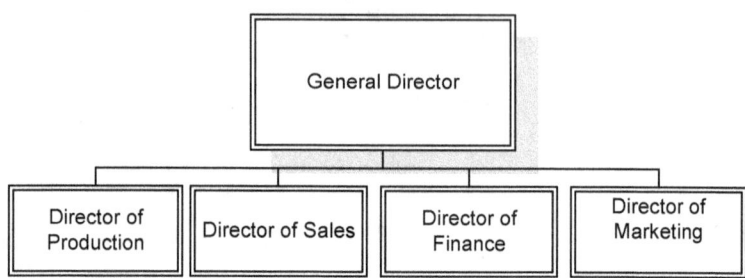

Figure 3. Functional organizational structure

Advantages: deepening specialization, improving the quality of management decisions; ability to manage multipurpose and multidisciplinary activities; reduced time of information flow; high competence of specialists responsible for performing specific functions; specialization of units on the performance of a certain type of management activity; top management is less loaded than with a linear structure; low administrative costs, absence of duplicated functions.

Disadvantages: lack of flexibility; bad coordination of actions of functional divisions; low speed of making managerial decisions; lack of responsibility of the functional managers for the final result of the enterprise; the difficulty of maintaining the constant interrelationships of various services; a high degree of conflict, a decrease in the responsibility of the performers for the work due to the fact that each performer receives instructions from several managers.

Linear-functional organizational structure

In a linear-functional control structure, the main relationships are linear and additional relationships are functional.

Advantages: unity and clarity of management; prompt adoption and implementation of decisions; personal responsibility of each manager for the results of the activity; redundancy in functional areas.

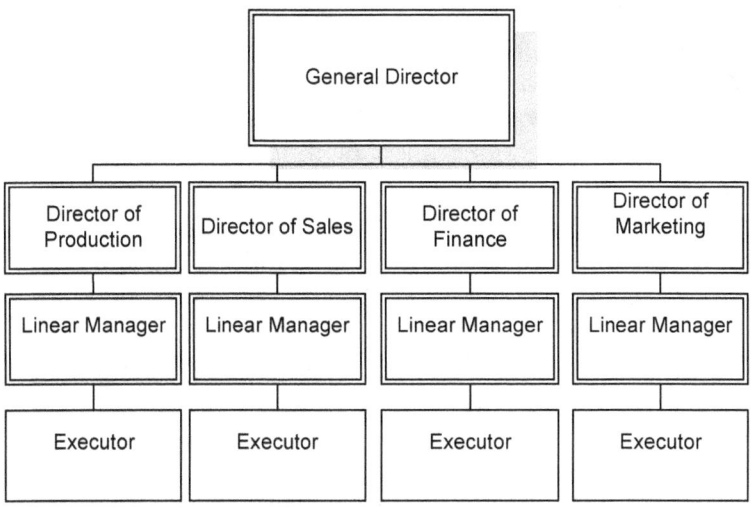

Figure 4. Linear-functional organizational structure

Disadvantages: disagreements between linear and functional services; counteraction of line managers to the work of functional specialists; misinterpretation of information transmitted to line managers by functional managers

Divisional organizational structure

In large firms divisional management structure is used to eliminate the shortcomings of functional management structures. The distribution of responsibilities is not by function, but by output or by region. In turn, divisional branches create their own supply, production, sales, etc. At the same time, prerequisites arise for unloading superiors by freeing them from solving current tasks. The decentralized control system ensures high efficiency within the individual departments.

Divisional management structure is based on the allocation of divisions. This type is currently used by most organizations, especially large corporations, since one can not squeeze the activities of a large company into 3-4 main departments, as in a functional structure. However, a long chain of commands can lead to uncontrollability.

Divisions can be allocated according to several criteria, forming the same structures, namely:

– product. Departments are created by product types. Polycentricity is characteristic. Powers for the production and marketing of a product are transferred to one manager. The disadvantage is the duplication of functions. Such a structure is effective for the development of new types of products. There are vertical and horizontal connections;

– regional. Departments are created at the location of the subdivisions of companies, if the firm has international activity. Effective for geographical expansion of market zones;

– consumer. Subdivisions are formed around a certain group of consumers. Effective to meet demand.

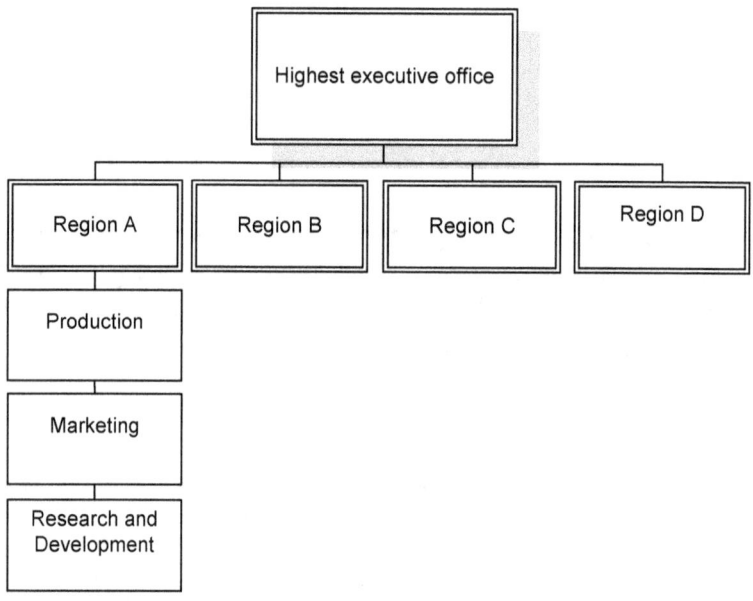

Figure 5. Divisional organizational structure

Advantages: close connection of production with consumers; ability to react quickly to changes in the external environment; better coordination of work in the units; increase the responsibility of the departments in matters of maximizing profits and gaining market share.

Disadvantages: the growth of the administrative apparatus; growth in expenses for management personnel; the complexity of information links; duplication of management functions in different divisions; struggle for resources between units.

Adaptive types

Project organizational structure

It is a temporary form of organization of the managerial process, created within the framework of solving a specific problem. At the end of the project, the specialists involved in its implementation, as a rule, return to permanent work in their units. All team members and resources allocated to the tasks assigned are subordinate to the project manager. The advantages of such a management structure include: high flexibility in organizing the production process, reducing the number of management personnel. Disadvantages can be called high requirements for the skills of specialists, the complexity of interaction of various projects within the company and the complexity of the development of the organization as a whole.

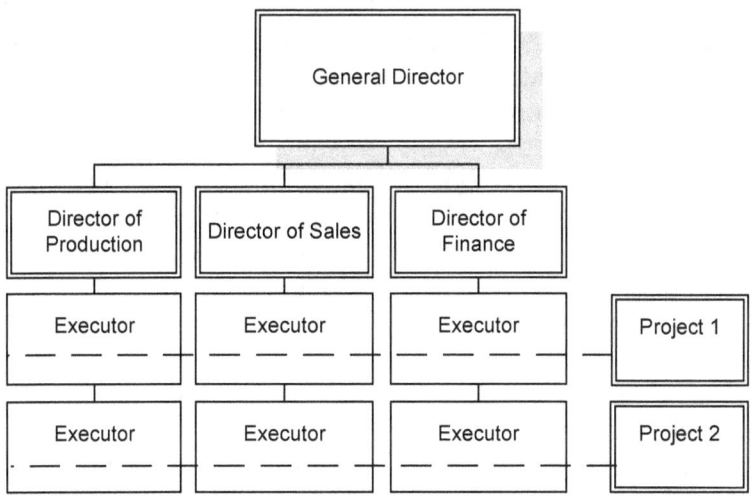

Figure 6. Project organizational structure

Advantages: flexibility, which allows to concentrate the activity of individual project managers on specific tasks;

Preservation of the principle of centralized production, because the head of the program is subordinated at the same time to the head of the enterprise; strengthening the personal responsibility of a particular leader for a particular project.

Disadvantages: very high requirements for the qualification, personal and business qualities of the project manager, who should not only manage all stages of the life cycle of the project, but also take into account the place of the project in the organization's network of projects; the need for fragmentation of resources, which complicates the development of production and scientific and technical potential as a whole; the formation of project groups that do not constitute sustainable education, which deprives workers of their awareness of their place in the organization and career growth; the problem of the employment of the released specialists.

Matrix organizational structure

It is one of the most effective type of the organization structure.

The essence of matrix structures is that temporary working groups are created in the operating structures, while the resources of the head of the group and the employees of other divisions are transferred to a double subordination.

With the matrix management structure, project teams (temporary) are formed, implementing target projects and programs. These groups are in a double subcategory, they are created temporarily. This achieves flexibility in the distribution of personnel, the effective implementation of projects. Disadvantages - the complexity of the structure, the emergence of conflicts.

Advantages: acceleration of introduction of innovations, personal responsibility of the project manager for the results of work; obtaining high-quality results for a large number of projects performed simultaneously; flexibility of the structure, allowing to distribute functional specialists between the projects; development of skills in decision-making in employees.

Disadvantages: the presence of double subordination, conflicts due to double subordination, the complexity of information links, lengthening the timing of decision-making due to the need for numerous approvals; growth of the administrative apparatus; the difficulty of acquiring the skills necessary for effective work in the team.

There are two main differences between the matrix and the project structure:

1. The matrix structure is a permanent formation;

2. In the matrix structure, employees are immediately subordinated to two leaders who are on the same level of the management hierarchy (managers with equal rights).

Integration organization structure

Integration structures are characterized by a combination of different types of organizational structures within a single enterprise.

Free organization structure

A free organization structure does not have any rigid organization, but acquires a particular structure, depending on changes in the conditions of the external environment or the tasks that are currently standing. Management under this type of organization is maximally decentralized, the hierarchical system is practically absent. The main advantage of such a structure is the ability to respond most effectively to highly competitive, constantly changing environmental conditions. At the same time, its main drawback is the extremely weak administrative controllability and the possibility of using it only in the conditions of high qualification of specialists.

Questions for self-examination

1. What is organization structure?

2. What types of organization structures are used by hotels?

3. What is the difference between bureaucratic and adaptive organizational structures?

Chapter 2. Organizational design

Organizational design (or design-management) is a tool for creating an effective organizational structure of an enterprise focused on the implementation of the strategy.

With the growth of the company, a situation inevitably arises when, together with the increase in turnover and revenue, the company grows a number of problems based on the interaction between departments and business units. When such problems become more and more, it is necessary to develop management systems of the company – approved rules of action for all employees and divisions of the organization.

Objectives of organizational design:
– development of organizational structures of the company as a whole or its various subdivisions;
– calculation of the optimal number of business units based on existing business processes and market practices;
– identification of responsibility areas for units;
– development of key performance indicators for the company as a whole and for individual units;
– determination of the degree of centralization for various divisions of the company.

Organizational design provides an increase in the level of controllability of the company; significant optimization of the organizational structure of the enterprise in accordance with the goals and strategies; distribution of powers, functions and responsibilities of certain employees based on the developed regulations; establishing the relationship between the organizational units of the enterprise.

Organizational design includes five basic blocks: (1) strategy (strategic vision, leadership policy, competitive strategy); (2) structure (distribution of power and responsibility, communication flows, organizational roles); (3) business processes and horizontal communications (building networks, teams, flexible structures and informal links); (4) the personnel remuneration system (material and non-material incentives); (5) human resources management (recruitment, selection, evaluation, training). That is, organizational design is not just about building an organizational structure, it's a more voluminous process.

Organizational design proceeds from the notion that it is

important not so much to keep a clear alignment of forces and distribute functions and powers, how to achieve synergy effect from the competent use of teams, the leadership potential of employees, the application of knowledge management methods, and the skillful use of information technologies.

The key concepts of organizational design are elements, relationships (relations), levels and powers.

Elements of the organizational system can be either individual employees (managers, specialists, employees), or services or bodies of the administrative apparatus, in which a certain number of specialists are engaged, performing certain functional duties.

The relationship between the elements of the management structure is maintained through relationships that are usually divided into horizontal and vertical. The first serve for coordination and are single-level. The second is a relationship of submission. The need for them arises in the construction of a hierarchical control system, i.e. in the presence of different levels of management, each of which pursues its goals.

Traditionally, in organizational design, the levels are distinguished – the top levels of management (management of the organization as a whole) and the lower levels (managers directly managing the work of performers). In large organizations, middle sections are formed, which in turn can consist of several levels.

In organizational design, linear and functional powers are distinguished. The first essence of the relationship is about the adoption and implementation of managerial decisions and information flow between the so-called line managers, i.e. persons fully responsible for the activities of the organization or its structural units. Functional links are associated with some or other management functions.

The requirements for the distribution of powers, the construction of communication systems, motivation and others depend on the stage of development of the organization itself. Obviously, the behavior of individuals and groups in a young company and its behavior in general is very different from their behavior in an aging company.

The life of any organization is divided into two stages: growth and aging. In the process of growth, it experiences the following stages of its development: bearing, infancy, childhood, youth, heyday, and stability. In the process of aging - the stage of aristocracy, the early bureaucracy, bureaucracy and death.

1. Bearing. This is the process of the birth of the organization. Physically, it is not exist yet, but there is a person (or a group of people) obsessed with a business idea.

2. Infancy. The company is formalized in fact. The main figure of the organization is its creator. As a rule, there is no formal organizational structure, no subordination, no appeal by name. There are no strict job descriptions.

3. Childhood (or «Come on!»). The organization's activities are stabilizing, the sales level is growing, the company is making a profit and can start spending money on development. The founder of the company becomes self-confident, appetites grow, the new opportunity is seen as a new priority. The company is characterized by reactive behavior, it reacts to new opportunities, but can not foresee them. The company develops through «trial-and-error».

4. Youth. This is a painful period in the life of the organization, which is characterized by a large number of contradictions and conflicts. The organization is expanding, new employees come with their values, norms, perceptions, conflicts arise. The stage of youth is characterized by a transition from intuitive to professional management, in the organization the main figure becomes a manager. The appearance of the manager leads to a change in the company's management system, redistribution of roles and responsibilities, more rigid formalization of relations, delegation of authority.

5. Heyday. The stage is characterized by an orientation toward the goal, a clear awareness of the institutional goals by the administration and the personnel of the organization. The organization has already formed a clear organizational structure, assigned official duties. An organizational culture has been created, new staff is selected taking into account the basic values and norms of the organization.

6. Stability. The company is strong, but loses its flexibility. There is less creativity, innovation, changes are not encouraged, comfort is seeking. The organization is still focused on the outcome, well managed, but increasingly conservative.

7. The aristocracy. This is the beginning of the aging of the organization. There is an increasing distance from customers, a

sense of self-preservation is escalating. Revenues are spent on strengthening the control system, insurance, on elements of prestige. A formalism is included in the custom of dress and circulation. The organization has considerable money resources, which are spent on letting the partners and rivals in the eye (expensive repairs, expensive equipment, cars, lush meetings, etc.). The organization creates a heavy moral and psychological atmosphere, the main thing is not what you do, but how you do it. Apathy is reigning, active employees do not like. The main quality that management values is loyalty to it.

8. Early bureaucracy. The company loses focus on results and customer satisfaction. On the part of the company it seems strong, but the leadership of the organization is obvious, first of all, financial. Open struggle begins, mutual accusations, search of guilty. The staff turnover is increasing.

9. Bureaucracy. This survival is for survival: the company can not adapt to the requirements of the external environment, there is no focus on the result, there is no need for changes, there is no command, but there is a system, rules, regulations. The information exchange is broken, the company collapses.

10. The death of the organization. No one expects anything from the organization. It can continue to exist for some time due to support from outside. If the company is completely dependent on customers, it dies.

All these stages are due to the conscious activity of individuals, the stages can be controlled (for example, to prolong the heyday due to strategy adjustment, reengineering, teamwork, etc.). At the same time, it should be noted that the organization can collapse at any stage of its development as a result of serious changes in the external environment, unfriendly absorption, changes in the interests and goals of the organization's owners, etc.

Questions for self-examination

1. What is organizational design?
2. In what stages the life of any organization is divided?
3. How to prevent the transition to bad stages of life cycle?

Chapter 3. Hotel organizational structure

Each hotel has its own organizational structure. For example, the reservation department can be part of the commercial department, the purchasing department can be subordinated to the financial department, the banquet service can be included in the food service. Sometimes the chef submits directly to the general director, and the food service manager commands only the waiters, and so on.

Depending on the category of hotel in the structure of its management, the corresponding units appear, for example, a business center, a fitness center, a doctor, a guest relation manager, butler service, etc. The approximate organizational structure of the hotel is presented on figures 7 and 8.

Small hotels have a much more simple management structure. However, the list of main divisions is preserved with their inherent functions. The simplest control structure in standard motels is, for example, the following: in a 100 rooms property, the director is directly managing four clerks of the reception and finance service, the head of the housekeeping service is managing eight maids, nine pages (bellman), and one repairman (electrical and plumbing works).

In large high-class hotels, on the contrary, the number of management levels increases: the general director, for example, has three deputies for the rooms, food and beverages and administrative services. The director of the room is managing the reception office (Front office), the housekeeping service (maids and cleaners of public premises, laundry, dry cleaning, etc.). The director of the food and beverages is managing the kitchen, restaurants, bars, banquet service, room service. The administrative director is managing the controller, the manager of the sales and marketing department, the chief engineer, the security service, the personnel department.

As the hotel owner can be: state, municipality, private owner, joint-stock company. Shareholders elect a board of directors (the number of members of the council elected from the shareholder, in proportion to the proportion of shares owned). The Board of Directors controls the work of the General Director, approves the financial plan (budget), listens to the CEO's report on its implementation.

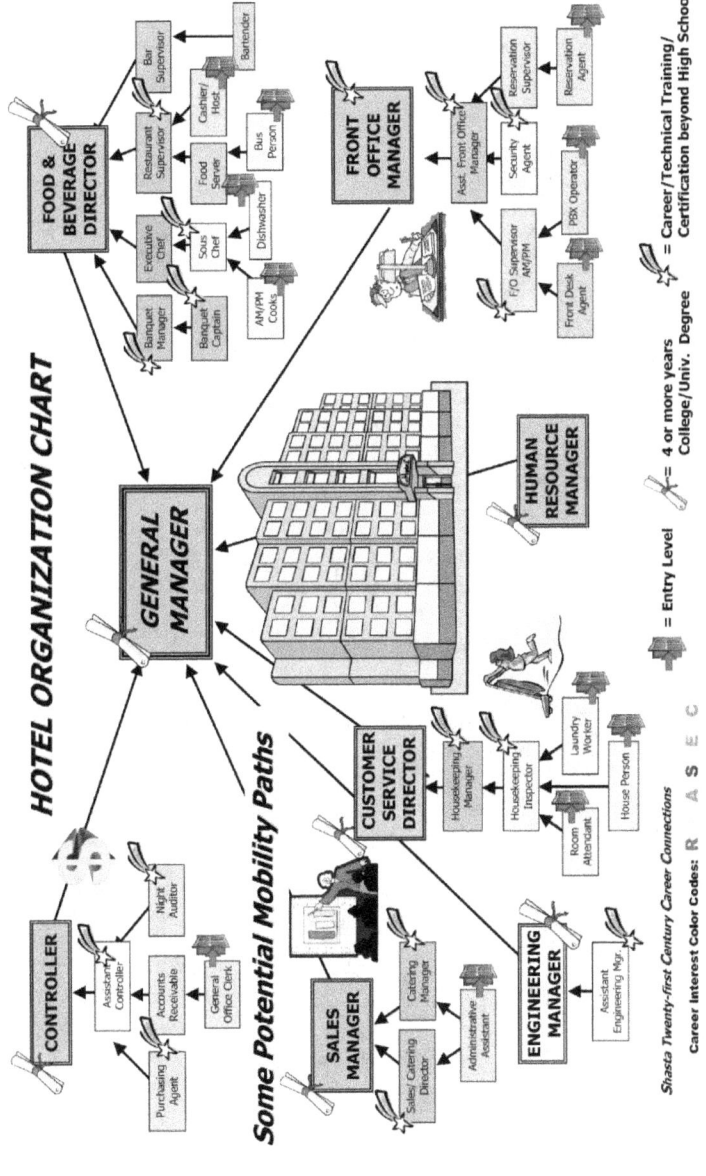

Figure 7. Hotel organizational structure with possible promotion (Source: http://housekeeping-hotel.blogspot.ru/2012/01/struktur-organisasi-hotel.html)

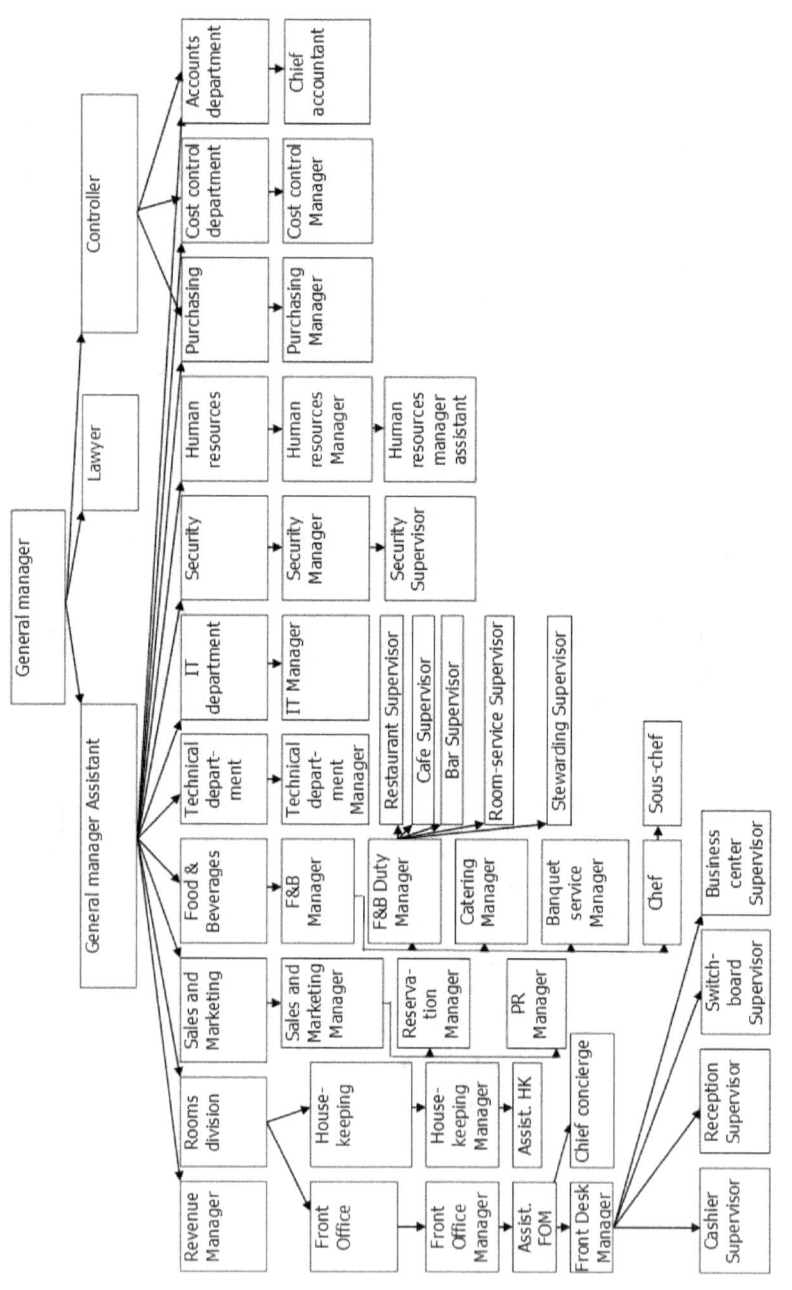

Figure 8. Full-service hotel organizational structure

The hotel divisions are grouped together in accordance with the chosen criteria. For example, the divisions of the hotel are divided into the main revenue generating (Revenue centers): rooms, restaurants, bars, and support centers: technical department, personnel department, accounting.

Widely used is the method of classifying hotel services on: front of the house and back of the house, which is based on the degree of contact of employees of a department of the hotel with customers. The reception, the restaurant refers to the front of the house, and the kitchen, accounting - to the back of the house. Employees of the latter group do not directly contact clients.

3.1. General Manager

The General manager (GM) is the first person in the hotel. He has any authority, sets the style of the hotel.

The GM has two main tasks:

– he must manage the hotel so as to fully satisfy all the wishes of the guest and thereby attract him to revisit the hotel;

– he must fulfill his duties to the owner of the hotel, ensuring its profitability.

In large hotels, the GM relies in his work on the board, which usually includes the heads of all major divisions of the hotel. The GM carries out daily operational management of the hotel staff, supervises the work of subordinates and solves all arising problems. Together with this, he must ensure and strategic management tasks. The GM submits to the Board of Directors the financial plan of the hotel and is responsible for its implementation. In addition to the annual plans, the GM is responsible for the development of a long-term (usually five-year) plan in which the company's long-term goals should be defined and strategies for achieving these goals developed. These strategies should be provided with appropriate financial, organizational and material resources.

Important tasks of the GM are also the development of a system of incentives and penalties for personnel and control over its observance. The General Director shall ensure normal working and resting conditions for the staff (timely provision of uniform, staff catering, dressing room equipment, rest rooms, etc.). Usually, before assuming the high post of GM, the employee should work in almost all the main divisions of the hotel.

3.2. Controller

The second person in the hotel management hierarchy is the controller. This is an employee, who combines the functions of chief accountant and financial director in one person. In large hotels, the controller functions are separated from the current control. And if the hotel enters the hotel chain, then the hotel controller reports not to the GM of this hotel, but directly to the headquarters of the chain. The functions of the controller include the development of a financial plan, accounting, auditing, all financial calculations of the hotel, etc. The controller must have a higher education in the specialty of accounting or related specialty.

3.3. Revenue Manager

The Revenue manager refers to the highest level of management of the hotel. He is responsible for the implementation of hotel revenue strategy for maximizing revenue through effective pricing and room management.

The Revenue manager reports directly to the GM and the regional revenue manager, if it is a hotel chain.

There are no direct subordinates of the Revenue manager as rule-lo. But under his leadership are the departments of reservation, sales and marketing of the hotel.

Key functional responsibilities are divided into the following main areas:

Strategic responsibilities are:

– development of a general price strategy in accordance with the overall strategy of the hotel, taking into account all market segments and distribution channels;

– formulation of the price structure, including the development of the provision on corporate rates, group rates for each group, wholesale prices, as well as evaluating the effectiveness of the price strategy taking into account competition in each market segment;

– effective management of the rooms fund and prices on all sales channels, including own site, third party sites and global reservation systems;

– cooperation with the sales managers and the head of the sales and marketing department in the issues of developing promotional campaigns and their pricing;

– creation of a logical price hierarchy for marketing promotions;

– monitoring of competitive prices and their impact on the performance of their hotel;

– development of guidelines for group sales of the hotel and their coordination with the management of the sales and banquet department;

– identification of periods of unsustainable hotel operation and development of a management plan in such periods in conjunction with the sales and marketing department, involving corporate and regional resources (in the case of a chain);

– tracking the market share and revenue level;

– analysis of competition reports using such tools as Deloitte & Touche, The Bench, Hotelligence and Market Vision.

Operational responsibilities include:

– responsibility for effective application of corporate standards, policies and procedures, including price plans, price categories, market segmentation, customer profiles and other issues of room management;

– tracking the needs for the application of all rates, timely extension of their properties in the automated hotel management system;

– ensuring the compliance of the best prices (BAR) in order to avoid any problems in them;

– ensuring the availability and correctness of information in internal and other electronic sales channels for a period of 500 days;

– administration of the revenue plan and the correctness of the indicators of hotel rooms in the management system;

– development of revenue forecast for 30, 60 and 90 days each month, as well as intermediate forecasts in the middle of the month;

– maintenance of accuracy of the forecast at a rate of 5%;

– preparation of a revenue management system in accordance with the annual budget (market analysis, competitive prices, quality and quantity of sales, etc.);

– ensuring the improvement of indicators for sales, close to full, i.e. in the amount of close to 95%. Sales at the level of 90-95% must be transferred to a level of over 95%, and sales of 95-97% in 98 and above;

– monitoring the revenue management system in conjunction with the sales department;

– weekly meetings on revenue and strategy, as well as participation in daily operational meetings;

– presentation of the hotel and its strategies at regional meetings (in the case of a chain).

Organizational responsibilities include:

– development of a plan for seeking, hiring, training and mentoring (if necessary) of the staff of the reservation department;

– conducting regular trainings to maintain the level of competence of employees and knowledge of current trends;

– participation in personnel reserve programs.

Technological duties include:

– ensuring understanding and implementation of all revenue management systems, including automation systems, such as OPERA, Fidelio, Internet systems, corporate reporting channels, revenue plan, corporate information exchange systems;

– detection of gaps in knowledge and skills of employees and preparation of applications for training programs;

– active participation in the selection or transition of the hotel to new software;

– verification of the correctness and regularity of data transfer to corporate management systems, including group forecasts and strategies in order to improve the effectiveness of working with groups.

Reporting responsibilities include:

– active analytical activity, concept and formation of strategic changes on the basis of available information: sales plan, statistics of rooms, groups, forecasts and reports of electronic consulting companies;

– active implementation of new opportunities for creating and analyzing reports.

Teaching responsibilities include:

– passing by himself of training courses such as «"Fundamentals of revenue management» and «Revenue planning», active search for new programs of professional development;

– passing additional courses as directed by the GM.

3.4. Rooms Division

Rooms Division includes a front office and housekeeping services. Rooms Division Manager is the head of this department and he is the one employee of this department.

Depending on the structure of a particular hotel, there can be no such service at all (for example, in small hotels), then both units are part of the Front Office.

3.4.1. Front Office

Front Office (FO) actually acts as one of the main services of the hotel. The head of this service acts as one of the main top-managers of any hotel. Front office is the place where the guest will get in with the hotel and leave it. For the guest – this is the face of the hotel. In addition, often all the communication of the guest with the hotel is limited to communication with the staff of this service.

The ability to communicate with a variety of people is an important quality of the employees of this service. They should be able to sell the hotel's products, create a favorable image, be a representative of the hotel management, be able to solve any guest problem, ensure its security, etc. The functions of FO include booking, registration, distribution of rooms, charging for accommodation, maintaining the necessary documentation and maintaining the database.

The structure of the service may be different.

Not all positions can be presented in every hotel. The hotel can also enter any other positions or reassign employees of other services.

A FO employee should be a good psychologist. The employee must thoroughly know all the information about the hotel (the advantages and disadvantages of each room, prices, location and opening hours of all hotel services), the city's attractions and ways of moving around it, the schedule of transportation, theaters, museums, etc.

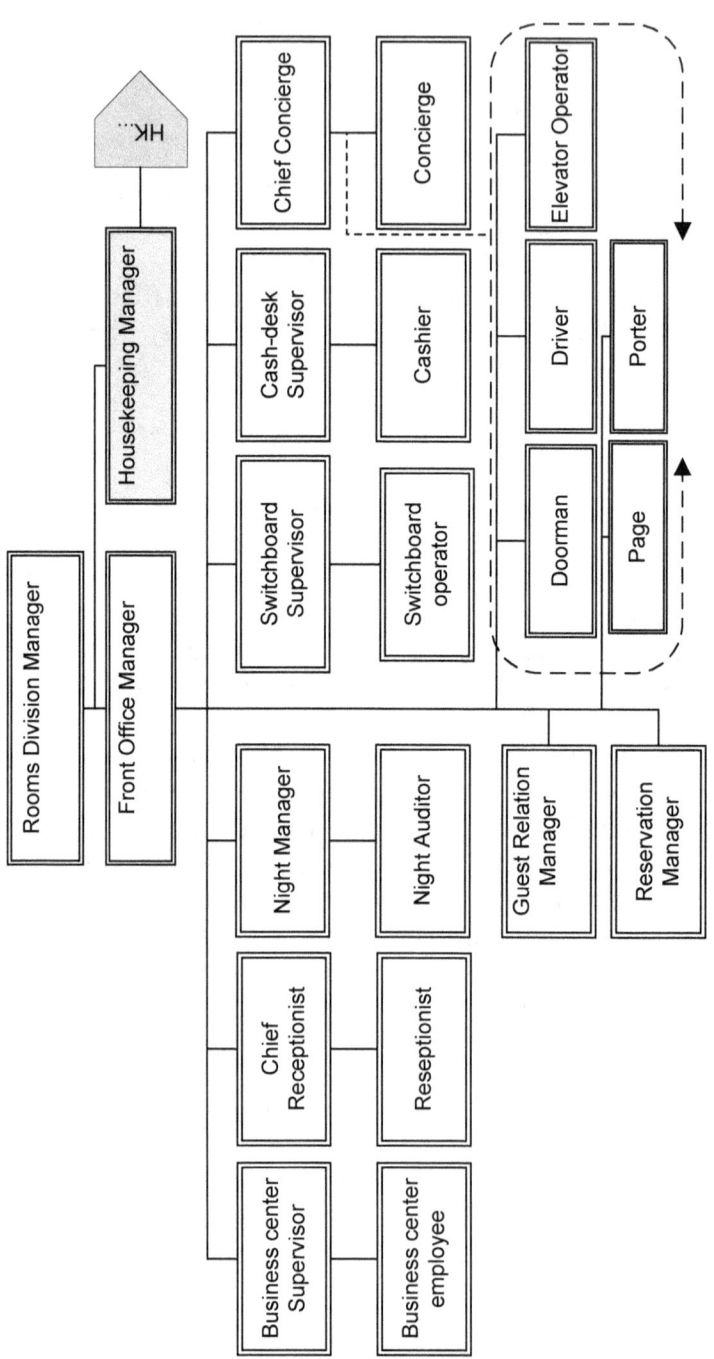

Figure 9. Hotel Front Office organizational structure

The main functions of the department are registration of visitors, distribution of rooms, settlement and issuance of clients and providing them with numerous additional services. It collects and stores information about customers, their tastes, preferences, birthdays. Information on guests and direct communication with VIP-clients is handled by the guest relation manager, the manager of the service or his deputy meets the most important guests, and the GM himself can also meet. In addition, the service can provide financial services (currency exchange, etc.), postal services, information about the city, weather, etc.

The service is located in the lobby of the hotel. It is desirable that employees can see elevators from their workplace. This allows for additional control over visitors and luggage. The service operates around the clock, usually in three shifts: from 7 to 15, from 15 to 23 and from 23 to 7 hours (it is possible to operate in two shifts for 12 hours, in this case, the staff schedule is 2 days after 2 days).

Night shift is shortened. The duties of the employee working on this shift include: summarizing the day, comparing them with the data of other sections of the hotel, preparing for the morning shift information on the status of the number of rooms (the number of free, booked, out of order rooms, how many guests will leave the next morning and how many will arrive). The night employee often performs the functions of a manager during his duty, however, in the event of difficult problems he must be able to quickly contact the real manager.

The service also includes a hotel cashier office, which is in double subordination – the reception and accounting service. A similar situation with the booking service – its work is controlled not only by the front office manager, but also by the manager of the marketing (commercial) department.

The function of the telephone service (Switchboard) includes: telephone calls, incoming and outgoing calls, control of payment for calls, wake-up calls, as well as answers to customer questions (or switching them to the information service).

Since the overwhelming number of contacts between guests and the hotel staff are for Front office employees, with proper preparation, they can have a significant impact on the increase in hotel revenues. To do this, special training is conducted for front office employees: to smile properly, to talk with the most difficult client and by phone, to avoid unwanted gestures and poses, etc. The service employee must be able to offer the client in time additional services, order a table in the restaurant, buy a more expensive room at the time of booking, reserve the room for the next visit, etc.

For senior management of the hotel, the FO presents daily reports on the occupancy (by rooms and beds) and on the actual average daily rate per room (and per bed). In addition, reflected income received for the day, made reservations and cancellations. Also important information about the guests (especially VIP categories). The forecast for the near future is also being developed. FO also deals with the resolving of conflict situations arising between the hotel and some guests.

Guest service

It is either a stand-alone unit or it is part of the Front office. The staff of this service works with customers in constant contact and performs the functions related to the service. The service manager is the manager, to whom doorman, bell man, luggage carriers (porter), lifters, concierges, couriers, drivers are subordinated. If there is no special manager, then the concierge coordinates the work of this service.

The doorman meets the guest, opens the door, calls a taxi, directs the parking lot, helps the guest to unload luggage, guards and passes it to the baggage carriers (porters) who bring it to the hotel and then carry them to the room. The doorman should also help the visitor to orient in the city, to know its main attractions, etc.

The page (bellman) accompanies the guest to the room, carries his hand luggage, opens the room, checks its readiness, explains the rules for using the equipment of the room to the guest, carries out the correspondence and do other functions of the bellboy. In addition, the page is the eyes and ears of the hotel's management: he must report all the suspicious cases he has seen.

Concierge

The first mention of the concierge dates from the XII century, called cumcerge (1192) or concierge (1220).

The original function of concierges was to support the

burning of candles in the castle. Later, the concierge added other responsibilities.

In 1929, in Paris, Pierre Quentin from the Ambassador Hotel founded an association of concierges to help each other, which included another 10 colleagues from the Grand Hotel Paris. In 1952, on April 25, Ferdinand Gillet organized the first international concierge congress at the Carlton Hotel in Cannes and the association was named the Les Clefs d'Or.

Until a certain time the concierges were not employees of hotels. They were independent entrepreneurs who bought the right to provide services to hotel customers. Currently there are both options.

Duties of the concierge:

– providing guests with all the necessary timely, reliable information about the hotel, the services provided, the events held;

– control of the list of guests, provision of VIP and provision of hotel services with this information;

– service orders for guests booking air, railway, bus, cruise tickets;

– receiving correspondence, checking it and sending it to rooms;

– acceptance of orders for car rent, taxi call;

– acceptance of orders for tickets to theaters, circuses, etc .;

– assistance in obtaining information concerning excursions, entertainment, allowing guests to choose the right services;

– assistance in emergency cases;

– execution of personal assignments of clients.

The concierge should have established contacts with any service partners, for example, excursion bureaus, car rental companies, travel agencies, etc.

It should be noted that concierge's services are free of charge. The encouragement lies on the guest. Do not forget this when you have some unusual requests, for example:

– the guest asked the concierge to drive his car to the hotel. The unusual request was that his car was parked in other city;

– the guest broke the toilet bowl in bathroom. He asked to buy a new one;

– the guest asked to organize a flight on a combat fighter;

– at 3 o'clock in the morning guest requested to find and buy

a bone for her dog;
- to buy seeds of capers bush;
- to attend a ballet school or a rehearsal in the theater;
- to dinner from only blue color dishes;
- saw the feet of the bed, table, chairs and cabinet by 4.5 cm;
- make sure that the sunlight rays in the room fall exclusively at an angle of 45 degree;
- Salvador Dali regularly stayed the hotel «Le Meurice», Paris, with his ocelot (ocelot – predatory mammal from the family of felines living in Latin America), urged to catch for ocelot insects in the garden of the Tuileries garden.

Night Auditor
At night the hotel sums up its operations for a working day. This is usually done in a period of time from 0.00 to 3.00 hours, because by this time all the services are completing their work and therefore the receipt of invoices from them to the cashier stops.
The most important duties are:
- all functions related to settlement, service, hotel guests' statement at night;
- entering data into customer accounts (which were not yet made by employees of other shifts);
- control the accuracy of charging payments for services provided to guests by previous shifts, making necessary adjustments, compiling a report on differences and mistakes for the head of the reception and accommodation service;
- maintaining the necessary documentation, parallel accounting;
- preparation of a full daily report on the activities of the hotel for the previous day
- preparation for 7.00 for morning shift of information about the occupancy of a rooms for the Housekeeping.

3.4.2. Housekeeping

This department is responsible for the cleanliness of the entire hotel and its rooms. Housekeeping Manager is in the head and usually has several assistants (senior maids, supervisors).

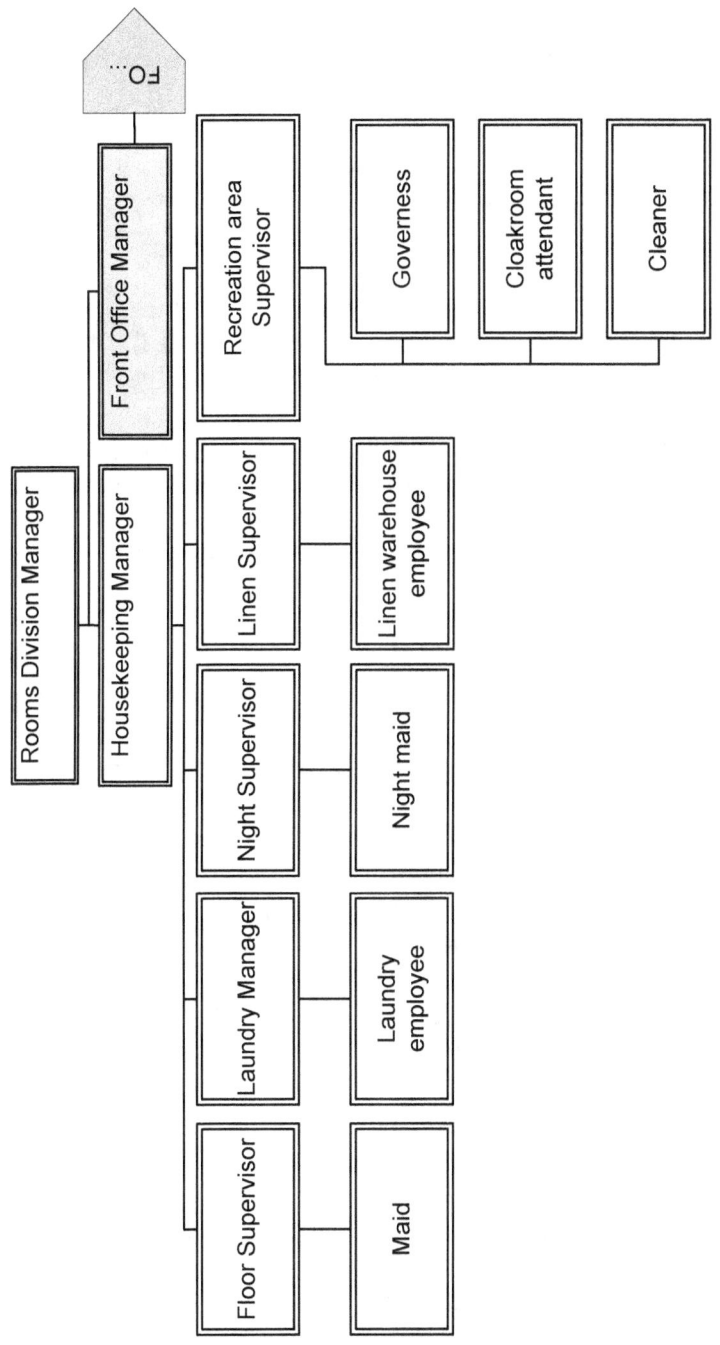

Figure 10. Hotel Housekeeping organizational structure

The senior maid is responsible for cleaning the rooms on one or two floors. The Housekeeping Department has a direct connection with the reception service and with the engineering service.

Housekeeping daily checks its data on the rooms with the data of the reception. The availability of the rooms is reported to the reception. The maids usually work in two shifts: from 7.00 to 15.00 and from 15.30 to 22.00. In hotels of high category, there is also a night shift.

The quota for one maid is 10-15 rooms per shift, depending on the class of the hotel, the size of the rooms and the type of cleaning (complete cleaning after the departure of the client or partial for the occupied room).

The room is cleaned from 20-30 minutes to 3 hours, depending on its size and equipment. However, the hotels set the standards themselves.

The quality of cleaning is checked by the senior maid or by duty manager.

There are special safety rules that must be observed by maids:

– do not open the door of the room to guests who forgot the key in the room, or workers;

– always keep the keys to the rooms to yourself, do not leave them on the working trolley;

– when cleaning the room, the door to it must be open, but the entrance is blocked by a working trolley;

– the maid should report suspicious customers.

For cleaning it is used special equipment and tools (vacuum cleaners, buckets on wheels, mops with pressure, ceiling brushes, brushes for radiators, brushes for the edges of the carpet, where dust is collected that is difficult to remove by a vacuum cleaner, sponges for washing dishes and a sponge and napkin, not leaving fibers, for glasses, etc.). Cleaning is carried out with the help of special chemical compounds for cleaning and disinfection, polishing for furniture, shampoos for carpets, carbon dioxide for freezing and removing chewing gum, pesticides for fighting insects, etc.

In addition to cleaning rooms for the service, the cleaning of halls, corridors, and restaurants is entrusted. This work is performed by special personnel using more heavy and powerful technology than the one that is designed for cleaning rooms. In addition to the daily in the hotels, periodic cleaning is carried out: washing the walls, cleaning and repairing furniture. Periodically, one or two rooms are put on renovation.

If the hotel has a games room with governesses, where clients can leave their children for a while, then this service is also part of the housekeeping.

The main employee of the housekeeping is a maid.

The duties of the maid include maintaining cleanliness of the hotel rooms, bathrooms, corridors, elevators and other assigned areas. General list of responsibilities and timetable for their implementation vary depending on the requirements approved in the hotel. Usually the maid:

– washing floors;
– vacuuming of carpets and soft furniture;
– wipes the dust from all surfaces including ceiling and walls;
– washes windows;
– watering flowers and rubs vases;
– veiled bed;
– change linen and towels;
– cleans the curtains;
– washing vases, decanters, soap dishes, mirrors, and other items;
– taking the guests orders for personal services rendered in the hotel and monitors the timeliness of their implementation;
– checks minibars in the rooms (if there is no a special service for minibars);
– checks equipment rooms;
– monitors the condition of the room and its equipment;
– checks a room and linen while guest's check-out.

The maid profession is predominantly female. Men wishing to work in this field is usually related specialty (for example, office cleaners, working on complex cleaning of the territory). The age limit for a maid every employer defines himself. In vacancy announcements meet the requirements from 18 to 55 years and even "the Maid should not be too young or too old."

Too young contenders for this position are often denied because they have little skills in cleaning. In addition, 18-year-old maids sometimes cause resentment among jealous wives, spoiling the family vacation. The lady is the retirement age with the responsibilities of the maid may not be able to cope physically: the work is quite heavy. In practice to get a maid really in any working age, if a woman has all the necessary qualities and has no medical contraindications.

Requirements

– physical endurance. This is the main requirement. Work of maid is physically hard, and the volume is big. In addition, it is sometimes necessary to work day in a row, including night;

– honesty. In the rooms you can store valuables, expensive equipment (cameras, laptops), jewelry, large sums of money. A maid can handle personal belongings (e.g., clothes). Cleaning is done in the absence of residents, but they don't have to worry about the safety of things left behind;

– sociability, friendliness, emotional stability, patience, courtesy, correctness;

– high level of personal hygiene;

– the lack of disgust. Maids have a lot of specific work — cleaning toilets, cleaning rooms and beds after stormy nights;

– diligence, punctuality, responsible attitude to work;

– developed observation and good visual memory. Without this, it will be difficult to monitor the condition of the room and the security of the hotel property;

– knowledge of a foreign language – at least at the basic level, in the amount of professional necessity. In large hotels serving foreigners, this requirement is required. In the rest – is an advantage.

The work of the maid is not recommended for people who have chronic diseases of the cardiovascular, nervous and endocrine systems, as well as respiratory organs, musculoskeletal system, joints, gastrointestinal tract, a significant decrease in visual acuity and hearing.

Particular attention is paid to the absence of skin diseases and allergies to chemicals. During cleaning, the maid is constantly in contact with a large number of various cleaning products. Rubber gloves do not always protect against strong substances. In addition, the maid has to at least inhale all the chemical compounds that are dispersed in the air. Also, poisonous spray cleaners can get into the eyes and other parts of the body.

Hotel linens in the laundry are processed with strong detergent powders and bleaches. The hands of the maids, who daily make dozens of beds, may suffer from developing allergies.

To work as a maid, there is enough general secondary education. The advantage of employing gives knowledge of a foreign language (mainly English), culture and customs of other countries, as well as special training.

In some hotels, the professional preparation of a maid is equated with... the presence of children. Personnel service believes that the best maids are obtained from experienced moms – they are not afraid of stress and any kind of cleaning.

But most often maids' training take place at the site of future work. It includes intro training (familiarity with the standards and technology of cleaning rooms, contents of the checklist, etc.). After the training, an internal examination can be followed, where the applicant must demonstrate firm bedding, the correct use of detergents, and the observance of the cleaning procedure.

Lately, zero experience has become a very significant plus. Modern hotel managers increasingly prefer personnel without work experience. The only exception is the maid's experience abroad, at a well-known international hotel. The maid's job is hard, but simple: after working for many years in this position, a person gets tired not only physically, but also morally, loses the impetus for perfection and enthusiasm.

Teaching maid «from zero» is often easier than retraining to the standards of a new hotel.

What the maid should know:
– all types of cleaning (daily, cleaning after departure, general, seasonal);
– rules of use and internal labor regulations in the hotel;
– prices for all types of paid services provided by the hotel;
– standards for equipping the premises and the hotel room;
– location of rooms, buildings, outbuildings;
– location of the stop valves;
– the rules for the use of vacuum cleaners, electric brushes, other electrical equipment used for cleaning;
– rules and norms of labor protection, safety precautions, industrial sanitation and fire protection;
– rules of ethics;
– regulations, orders, methodological and other guidance materials on the issues of hotel services.

The modes of work of maids in each hotel can vary greatly:

– day shifts (12 hours each) – two days after two;
– night shifts (12 hours each) – a day through three days;
– five working days in a row from 9 to 18 hours;
– for weeks – each maid works in one shift for a week, then shifts to another shift;
– on sliding schedules – the maid passes from shift to shift on certain days of the week.

In any case, the total working time should be no more than is in labor laws (for example, 40 hours per week).

The salaries of maids are very different. Payment depends on the set of responsibilities, the level the hotel, the geographical location of the hotel and many other factors. On average, the maid of a good Moscow hotel earns 2 Euros per hour. In Europe, the lowest rate for a maid is 7.87 Euros per hour.

Sometimes a good additional income of maids make up a tip. In different countries, guest should (not must) leave from 0.5 Euros to 10 Euros a day.

In addition, in many hotels, the maid is entitled to free meals. Some hotels offer free English language courses for staff.

Career prospects for the maid are slim. As part of her position, she can improve her qualifications and master related specialties. Experienced maid can claim the promotion – senior maid. She supervises the maids, monitors the quality of their work, is responsible for the availability, exchange, accounting of linen and detergents on the floor. To further advance up the career ladder of the hotel business, higher education is already required in this area.

Pros of the maid:
– maids have stable demand in the labor market;
– work does not require special education;
– it is easy to get job without work experience;
– uniforms are provided (which means that the cost of working clothes is reduced);
– often the employer provides employees with food, sometimes even accommodation;
– a woman who has worked as a maid becomes a cleaning professional, which is very useful in the management of her own household.

Disadvantages of maid work:
– work is hard physically;

– work is not easy psychologically. Since the cleaning is done in the absence of customers, the maid seldom hears words of gratitude. But the anger of a guest practically for any reason falls first of all on the maid. Often, clients suspect maids in theft, and most often – without foundation;

– work is not very promising;

– if the maid does not notice damage caused by the eviction of the guests (broken dishes, stolen towels, broken electrical appliances, substitution of bottles in the mini-bar), compensation will be deducted from her salary.

– the maids work under constant supervision: the quality of cleaning is checked by both clients, the senior maid, and the quality control service (sometimes under the guise of an ordinary guest). For the shortcomings, maid can lose a substantial part of the salary.

What the maid should and should not do

Garbage. Empty all garbage baskets and tanks. Any item left in them should be considered «discarded», which means it can be removed from the room. Any items that are too large for a garbage container (for example, pizza boxes), but located on or near it, can also be treated as garbage. If you are not sure, leave it until the guest leaves.

Often, the maids mistakenly take as a garbage the empty boxes left next to the trash can. For example, in one hotel the maid threw a box from the laptop purchased by the guest, the guest noticed the loss only a day later when he wanted to return the laptop that did not suit him back to the store. As a result, the guest demanded compensation from the hotel for the incident.

Clothing. Any clothes guest thrown on the floor, under the bed or any other piece of furniture, you can neatly fold and leave on the dresser, desk or on the bed. Shoes can be corrected and expose along the baseboard, where the guests about it will not stumble. Do not put shoes and hang clothes in a closet, fold in a box or in a suitcase. Things should remain in the mind of the owner. This problem is one of the most common, as guests often forget things in drawers and cabinets, especially if they did not put them there.

Toiletries. During the cleaning of the sink and bath, the maid can fix the personal hygiene units of the guest. Toothpaste and brushes can be put in an empty glass so that they do not come into contact with the dressing table. Brushes for hair, combs and cosmetics can be spread out on a hand towel, and bottles with shampoo and conditioner put on the edge of the bath. However, never put personal hygiene items back in the guest's cosmetic bag. There are cases when the guests accused the hotel of theft because of the loss of expensive cosmetics, and after the received compensation they found the missing things in their cosmetic bag or other place not used for storing cosmetics.

Do not touch this

Values, electronics and medicine. Never touch money, jewelery, keys, electronics or the medicines of a guest. Moving or touching these objects, you can incur the suspicion of dishonest intentions. Despite the warning of hotels that they are not responsible for valuables left outside the safe, complaints about the loss of jewelry and expensive accessories are quite common. Sometimes the guests specifically provoke the staff in the hope of getting compensation for the damaged or missing jewelry.

In one hotel, the maid mistakenly threw the empty (as it seemed to her) box from the medicine, in which there were several expensive and, most importantly, vital tablets for the guest. The hotel could hardly organize the delivery of a rare medication, but in the opposite case, everything could end more tragically. Also among the guest reviews there are complaints that the maids change / close / open / use the guests' electronic devices.

Boxes, suitcases, wallets, briefcases and bags. Do not move, look, open or put things in guests' drawers, purses, briefcases, or any kind of bags. Again, such actions can be perceived as potential theft. Wardrobes can be opened only for the replacement of laundry bags, forms for washing and dry cleaning, or to return to the place of the ironing board and iron.

The guest of one hotel accused the maid in the breakdown of the celebration of her anniversary because she forgot in her room a clutch with precious earrings specially ordered for the evening dress, which the maid put carefully into the drawer of the dresser. When leaving, the guest did not check the drawers of the dresser, as she was sure that she did not use them.

Glasses or cups with contents. Never empty and do not wash cups, mugs or plastic cups that contain contents, even if it's water. Guests can often leave there contact lenses or precious jewelry. After pouring liquid from these containers, you can inadvertently get rid of objects belonging to the guests.

Among the complaints – there are cases when maids poured water with lenses lodgers or took water for medicinal preparations of guests. In order not to face such problems, do not forget to prescribe in the standards, these obvious, at first glance, rules.

It is important for the manager to check how much the service personnel knows, understands and follows all the rules and standards. Monitoring compliance with these requirements is much easier than solving problems and combating negative feedback.

Other staff of Housekeeping

Manager of the laundry. Responsible for the work of laundry and chemicals. He is a deputy manager of housekeeping. Responsible for high-quality timely cleaning of linen, towels, tablecloths, napkins for food structures, for the work of their staff (laundress), for compliance with the budget.

Supervisor of a warehouse of linen. Responsible for the work of the warehouse.

Supervisor of recreational areas. Responsible for all recreational areas of the hotel company: swimming pools, saunas, fitness centers, play areas.

3.5. Technical (engineering) department

The modern hotel is full of sophisticated engineering equipment (high-speed elevators, air conditioning, heating, water supply and sewerage systems, electric and gas kitchen equipment, cable TV, computers, etc.).

Small hotels often can not afford to maintain a full engineering staff for the maintenance and repair of all equipment. In this case, the hotel contracts with specialized companies that carry out its maintenance and repair. The engineering service in this case has a relatively small staff of station wardens capable of eliminating simple faults in the plumbing and electrical equipment and performing competent operation of the entire equipment.

In large modern hotel companies, the organizational structure of the engineering service is quite extensive.

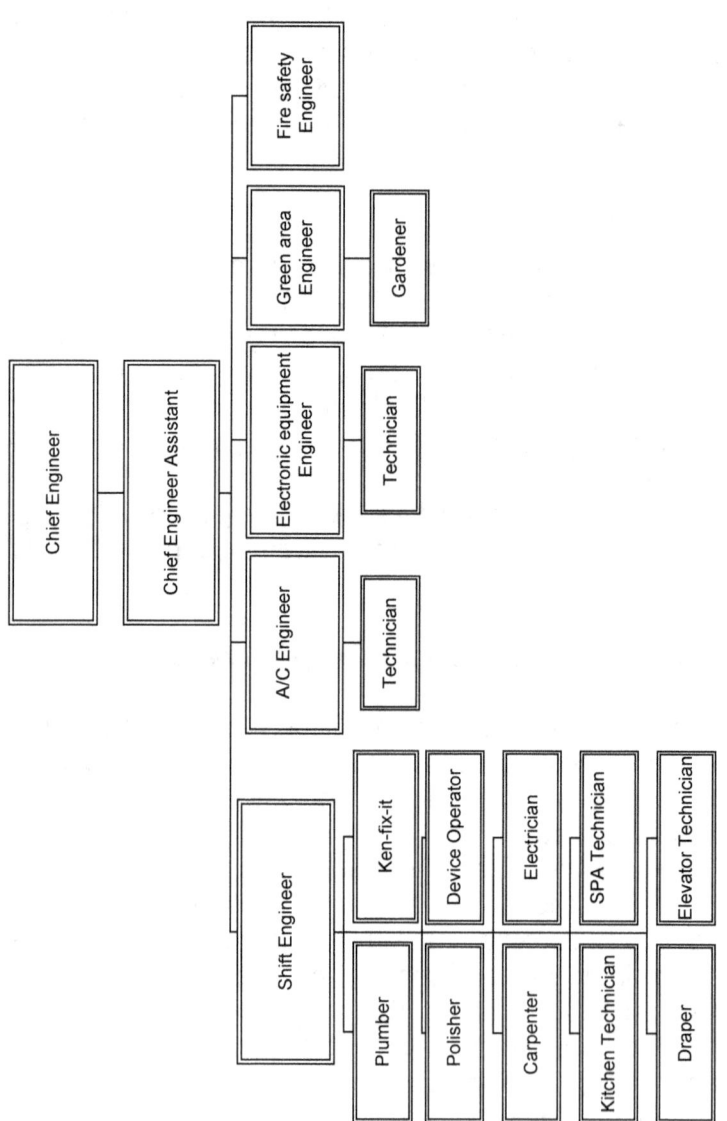

Figure 11. Hotel Technical department organizational structure

The chief engineer is in charge of the technical department (he may be called chief engineer, director of building operations, building superintendent, or some other combination of these words). The chief engineer is subordinated directly to the GM.

The duties of the chief engineer include:

– determine the technical policy, development prospects of reconstruction and technical re-equipment of the hotel;

– ensuring a constant increase in the level of technical readiness of the state to operate, reducing labor costs, improving the quality of service and efficient use of production assets;

– maintenance of uninterrupted functioning of systems of power supply, heating, hot and cold water supply, the water drain, ventilation and air-conditioning, serviceability of fire extinguishing means;

– maintenance of a constant technical serviceability of all technological equipment, freight and passenger lifts;

– maintaining the proper technical condition of buildings and facilities, monitoring compliance with all employees of the enterprise safety rules and fire safety regulations;

– organization of works on introduction of advanced technologies;

– maintenance, repair, modernization of equipment;

– control over observance of schedules and quality of works on capital and current repair of buildings and equipment;

– providing preparation for work in the autumn-winter and spring-summer seasons;

– control over efficient and rational use of fuel, energy and other resources;

– organization and control of production training of technical personnel, observance of labor and production discipline;

Duty (Shift) engineer is subordinated to the chief engineer. His duties include:

– ensuring uninterrupted operation, proper operation, repair and modernization of equipment, electrical and thermal networks, air lines and gas pipelines;

– determination of the need for fuel and energy resources;

– preparation of justifications for technical re-equipment;

– drawing up applications for the purchase of equipment, materials;

– participation in consideration of causes of accidents and development of measures for their prevention;
  – testing of protective equipment;
  – technical supervision of devices;
  – monitoring compliance with operating instructions, maintenance and supervision;
  – control over the performance of capital and other repairs.

Engineer for climatic equipment (A/C) responsible for:
  – temperature monitoring;
  – development of maintenance schedules for climate equipment;
  – maintenance of work and timely maintenance of climatic equipment.

Territory Engineer (Green area engineer) responsible for the operation of all equipment located on the territory of the state complex (irrigation system of the garden, etc.)

Fire Safety Engineer. At small enterprises an individual fire engineer is not required. For fire safety GM is responsible. Duties of a fire safety engineer:
  – development of internal regulatory documents on fire safety;
  – briefing of employees;
  – control compliance with fire regulations;
  – formation of fire prevention plans and their implementation;
  – conducting inspections (in conjunction with an officer of the Ministry of Emergency Situations).
Fire is a fairly common phenomenon in the hotel business. The main reasons for the fire in the hotel: smokers, defective electric and kitchen equipment, fireplaces, chemicals in the warehouse, fire debris. The fire safety system includes a fire alarm system in all areas of the hotel, fire extinguishing means (fire hoses, fire extinguishers, etc.), evacuation means (fire ladders), as well as regular training activities for personnel. All rooms must be provided with evacuation schemes in case of fire. All hotel staff must be firmly aware of their actions in case of fire.

Ordinary employees of technical department include a whole

range of professions: electricians, plumbers, elevator staff, technicians, gardeners, etc.

The engineering service can include whole workshops for furniture repair, carpets, and also room repair service (painters, polishers, draperies, etc.). All works performed by this service are registered in a special journal.

3.6. Food & Beverages department

Most hotels have a very branched structure of F&B. The main types of services include:

1. Food for the personnel (Employee dining);
2. Minibar service;
3. Restaurants (including a gourmet restaurant);
4. Coffee Shop;
5. Conference and banquet service (Conferencing & Banqueting)
6. Outside catering service;
7. Room service;
8. Bars;
9. Service in the lobby (Lobby, Lounge).

Table 2.
F&B in different types of hotels

5*	Coffee Shop, Gourmet Restaurant, Specialized Restaurants, Bar, Lobby Bar, Catering, Room Service (24 hours), Executive Lounge, Minibar, Cafe by the pool, Meals for staff, Room equipment
4*	Coffee Shop, Specialized restaurant, Bar, Lobby bar, Banquet service, Minibar, Meals for staff, Room equipment
Mid-scale hotel	Buffet breakfast, Bar, Vending machines, Meals for staff
B&B	Breakfast, limited meals on the menu at the set time or on request
Hostel	Snack bar, Vending machines

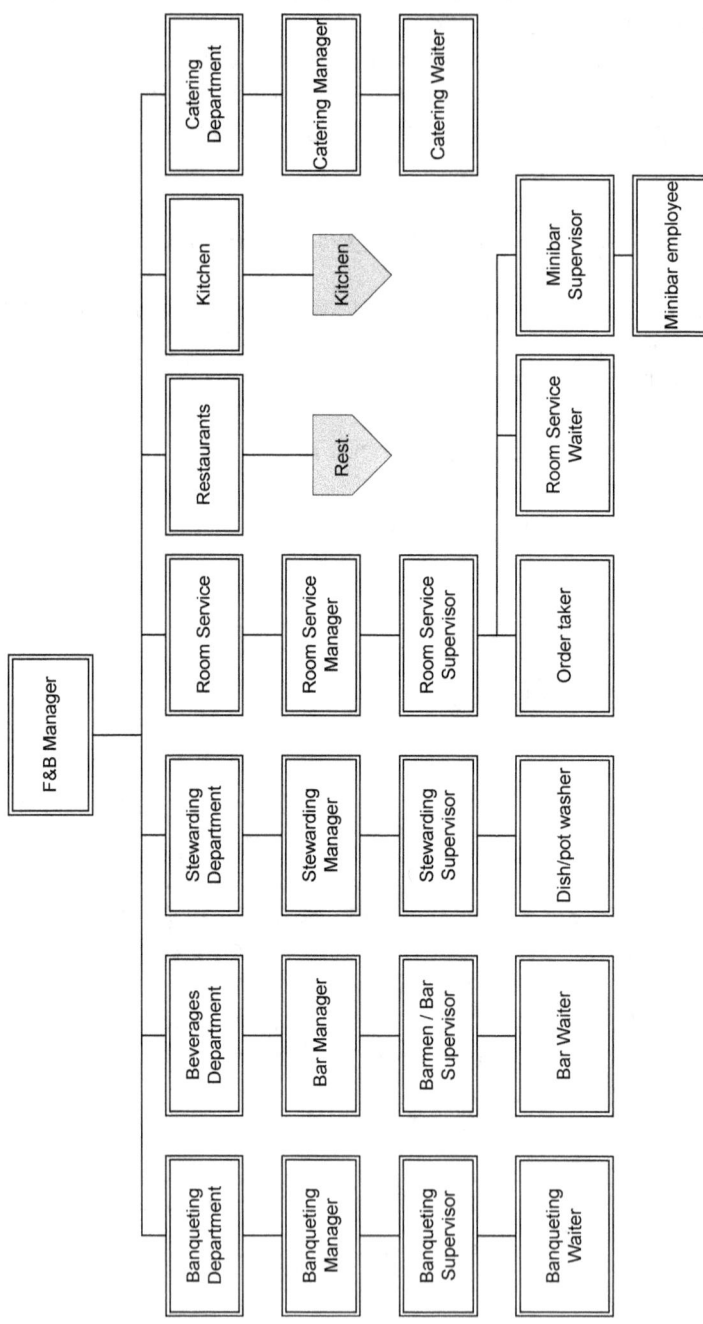

Figure 12. Hotel Food & Beverages department organizational structure

F&B Manager is the head of this department. His duties are:
– managing of restaurant service;
– managing events to increase revenue;
– develop and maintain a budget, an action plan to promote the department to stimulate sales and revenue, while controlling costs;
– research, review and analysis of competitors, market trends, commentaries and customer needs;
– provision of appropriate personnel, training, motivation, coaching, counseling and development of the team team;
– assess changes in guest needs and competitiveness in order to recommend the appropriate product/service;
– eEnsuring the satisfaction of guests and employees, while maintaining competitive ability in the market and exceptional financial performance

Banqueting Manager:
– participation in negotiations with the client, consulting;
– help in choosing the design of the restaurant, placing guests;
– planning of necessary equipment and equipment;
– preparing the restaurant for a banquet;
– instructing staff, including waiters and cooks;
– organization of necessary purchases;
– organization of table layout;
– quality control of cooked meals;
– putting the hall in order after the event.

Catering Manager performs the same duties as the bankueting manager, but is somewhat wider. The peculiarity of his work is organization and equipment for a banquet on often unprepared grounds, equipping with necessary equipment, gathering and organizing a team of attendants, importing the necessary products, textiles, utensils, inventory.

He must plan where the technical and guest areas, animation stations, musicians will be located. On the day of the event, he must monitor the order, the work of waiters and cooks.

At the end of the event, the banqueting manager should bring the restaurant or the playground to order, organize garbage collection, provide logistics and safety of the exported equipment,

equipment, utensils.

Manager of beverages department is responsible for:
– inventory, seizure of unsuitable beverages;
– price negotiation with suppliers;
– pricing based on regulatory returns;
– sales reports;
– prevention of losses, frauds;
– scheduling of shifts of employees;
– control of labor discipline;
– control compliance with certification and other requirements for beverages and employees.

Bar Supervisor / Barman / Bartender should know:
– the structure and layout of the restaurant, cafe, bar;
– standards of equipment and furnishing of restaurant premises;
– types of service;
– types of dishes, glasses, cutlery, napkins, tablecloths;
– principles and technologies for serving dishes;
– psychology of product promotion and sales;
– product types, assortment;
– methods and methods of making menus, cards of wines and drinks;
– fundamentals of restaurant marketing and sales theory;
– special language on the subject of catering services;
– the theory of interpersonal communication;
– needs and expectations of customers;
– protocol and etiquette;
– rules for preparing documentation for public catering;
– standards of record keeping;
Official duties:
– coordinates the work of the bar staff to clean the restaurant, cafe, bar to the working day;
– coordinates the work of the attendants in preparing the halls for the servicing of visitors (table setting, preparation of equipment for spacing and feeding food, drinks); creation of comfortable conditions (temperature and visual);
– coordinates actions for meeting and greeting visitors, controls the quality of customer service by the staff of the bar

(administrators, waiters, etc.).

– supervises the acceptance of orders by the staff (order and procedure of presentation by the waiters of the menu, wine cards, beverage cards, helping customers in choosing food and drinks, offering special and specialty dishes to customers, accepting the order);

– monitors the order, procedure and sequence of customer service, observance of food technology and service rules in accordance with each type of service, various ways of serving dishes, serving wines, alcoholic and nonalcoholic beverages;

– controls the preparation of the customer's account and acceptance of payment;

– works with customer complaints;

– carries out the control over observance by the personnel of a bar of standards of hygiene, maintenance of sanitary cleanliness of the equipment and stock;

– carries out the control over preparation of restaurant, cafe, a bar to the termination of the working day;

– plans the needs of the bar;

– organizes the instruction of the bar staff, distributes tasks between them and determines the degree of their responsibility;

– participates and coordinates the work on the preparation of the menu, on the design of the halls of the bar.

Stewarding Manager responsible for the cleanliness and performance of all F&B equipment:

– maintenance of sanitation standards for all premises and cooking areas;

– serviceability and cleanliness of kitchen equipment and F&B services;

– staff training and ensuring its compliance with hotel standards;

– minimization of costs;

– development and implementation of the strategy of the stewarding department;

– ensuring coordination of department activities with other departments.

Room Service includes a manager, supervisors, waiters, as well as mininbar staff, who are engaged in checking and replenishing the minibar in the guest rooms.

Room service manager is responsible for:

– personnel management: selection, training, adaptation, motivation, control of correct and precise fulfillment of the functional duties of the officials;

– makeing a schedule for the work of the waiters;

– distributing the amount of work;

– monitoring the correct serving of tables, trays;

– checking the correctness of the formation of orders under the menu room service;

– budgeting and financial reporting on the services provided, increasing profitability, budget execution;

– the solution of the arising conflict situations.

Waiter of Room Service except for the usual duties of the waiter is still responsible for the timely collection of dirty dishes from floors

Supervisor of the minibar is responsible for:

– ordering products from the warehouse;

– distribution of the scope of work;

– scheduling the work of employees of the minibar;

– reporting.

Minibar employee is responsible for:

– checking the minibars and replenish them in the guest rooms;

– crediting the consumed food and drinks to the guest's bill;

– blocking of minibars in case of guest debt;

– checking the technical condition and operating mode of the minibar.

In general, the employee of room service should know the products offered to guests, a wine card; know the menu of each period of the day (breakfast, day menu, night menu); help guests when choosing an order; know the prices of drinks and cocktails; know the menu with all the ingredients in different languages; know the cooking time of all dishes.

3.6.1. Restaurants

Restaurant Manager is the head of each restaurant in hotel.
Restaurant manager is responsible for the organization and administration of all services.

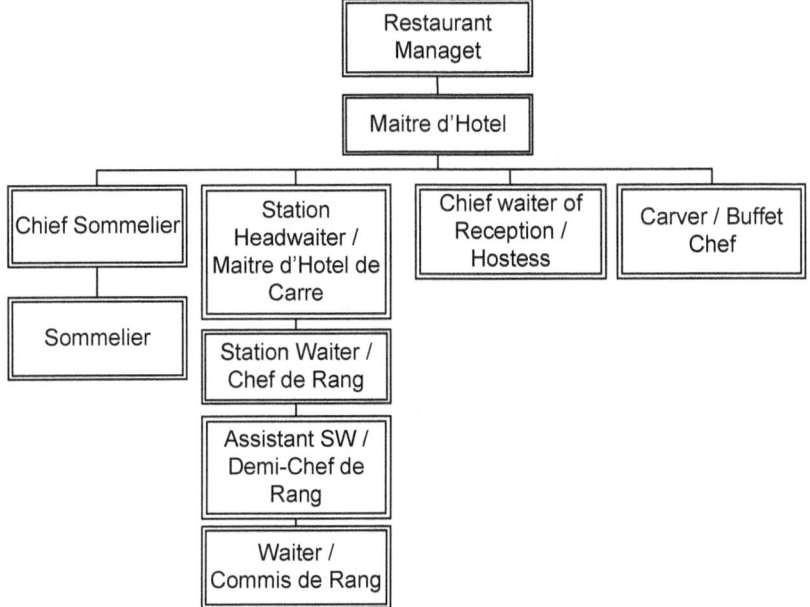

Figure 13. Restaurant organizational structure

His duties are included:
– hiring, training and supervision of employees;
– provision and regulation of all business processes;
– provision of customer requests;
– scheduling of employees;
– control of staff performance;
– monitoring of equipment and items, timely ordering and receiving;
– ensuring sanitary and hygienic standards;
– control over observance of service standards and food preparation processes;
– control over observance of rules and norms of occupational safety and health;
– control over the shelf life of products, inventorying;

– maintenance of cash records, collection of cash;
– prevention and resolution of conflict situations with the participation of visitors and employees of the restaurant.

Chief waiter (Headwaiter / maître d 'hôtel / supervisor).

Initially, the term «maître d'hotel» (from the French «owner of the hotel») was used in France to refer to the owners of inns at postal stations. Passengers here did not stay for a long time, and stopped only to rest and have dinner. The maître d'hotel host accepted them. He seated visitors in the dining room at a common table, accepted their orders and handed the servants to the kitchen, counting them.

During the whole working day the headwaiter is in the restaurant hall. He meets visitors at the entrance to the restaurant, helps them to stay in the hall, creates a good mood for them, provides a pleasant atmosphere and a reputation for the conduct. The headwaiter is perfectly familiar with the menu and wine list of his restaurant or cafe, so he can advise visitors some dish or a wine brand. He must know the technology of cooking, the order of their presentation.

Duties:

1. Organization of the restaurant hall:
– organization of interaction with all structural divisions of the restaurant;
– organization of the work of the staff; planning and monitoring the working time of employees;
– planning and control of the required stock of restaurant linen, dishes, appliances and accessories;
– control of the preparation for the work of the restaurant hall and ancillary rooms;
– observance of sanitary rules and hygienic standards, rules for the protection of labor and fire safety;
– inventory of table linen, dishes and appliances;
– instructing staff at the workplace;
– registration of documents and maintenance of the corresponding records management).

2. Organization of the meeting and greeting of the guests:
– development of the procedure for meeting, seating and farewells to visitors;
– control of staff communication with guests;

– consultation and assistance in the choice of food and drinks; creation of comfortable conditions for visitors.

3. Quality control of visitors in the restaurant:

– control of the procedure for welcoming guests, offering menu, receiving and executing an order, serving guests, preparing an account and accepting payment;

– control of holding banquets, cleaning tables; compliance with protocol and etiquette;

– prevention of conflict situations.

4. Work with restaurant visitors:

– the formation of a positive image of the restaurant;

– creating a pleasant and friendly atmosphere;

– study of consumer preferences of restaurant visitors;

– preparation of proposals and their implementation to improve the service of visitors;

– establishment and expansion of relations with the public and mass media;

– accounting and analysis of complaints, claims and wishes of visitors; elimination of deficiencies in the work of the restaurant; compliance with protocol and etiquette rules.

5. Drawing up a map of wines and beverages.

6. Selection of restaurant accessories and other goods from suppliers based on available information and market research data.

7. Sales management in the restaurant hall:

– control of the availability of necessary stock for the stable operation of the restaurant hall;

– control and analysis of sales of food and drinks in the restaurant;

– definition of consumer preferences and rating of the most popular dishes and drinks;

– training the staff in the right combination of food and drinks.

8. Work with personnel and evaluation of its activities:

– selection and placement of restaurant staff;

– distribution of responsibilities and delegation of authority;

– scheduling the work of restaurant staff;

– increase of labor motivation of the personnel on the basis of application of socially-psychological methods of management and material stimulation;

– development of organizational culture and improvement of official etiquette;

– the solution of social and psychological conflicts and problems.

9. Conducting professional trainings in the workplace.

10. Introduction of progressive methods of work organization.

Chief sommelier (Headwaiter for wines) has the organization of customer service in terms of providing a sufficient range of alcohol and tobacco products as a main task.

Duties:

– selection of suppliers of cigars, wines and spirits, their purchase; making of wine and cigar cards; organization of proper storage of wine and sigar;

– providing visitors with complete information on various beverages and cigars; recommendations for choosing beverages;

– decanting (the process of slow transfusion of wine from a bottle into a canter – a special glass vessel – to saturate the wine with oxygen), the supply of wine, liqueurs and other spirits;

– training of waiters for serving wine;

– settlements with visitors.

– maintenance of reporting documentation; reports on the movement and balance of goods;

– ordering, acceptance and control of the presence of wines and alcoholic beverages in the warehouse, items obtained from the warehouse;

– maintenance of a proper sanitary condition of a restaurant hall, an auxiliary premise, the trading-technological equipment and stock;

– check the medical examinations of personnel.

Station headwaiter / section supervisor.

In large restaurants, the trading floor is divided into zones (sections). Each zone consists usually of 4-8 tables. The station hedwaiter of the zone is responsible for its work.

Duties:

– accepting orders;

– provision of customer service;

– assistance to the chief waiter (headwaiter);

– organization of work of the employees of the zone;

Reception headwaiter:
– taking orders for table reservations;
– reservation of tables and placing on zones of restaurant;
– welcome guests upon arrival;
– seeing off guests to the tables and seating.

Carver / buffet chef / chef at breakfast.
This is the chef who is in charge of the buffet at breakfast. He cooks at a party and is responsible for slicing.
Duties:
– making offers on dishes offered at breakfast;
– making proposals for the type of kitchen;
– help in developing the menu;
– making changes to the menu «on the fly»;
– development of recipes for dishes, checking the compliance of cooked dishes with recipes;
– preparation of various types of dishes;
– control the filling of the pantry table.

In addition to the above positions, there may also be:

Barista
Barista (italian – barista) – literally «a man working at a bar stand», a barman, a coffee brewer, a coffee maker who knows how to make coffee or drinks on his basis and send it to the visitor. In other words, it is a person performing functions bartender, but not working with alcohol and cocktails, and with coffee or drinks based on coffee.
Duties:
– knowledge of the rules of coffee preparation;
– comprehensive understanding of coffee blends: knowledge of coffee varieties, places of growth of grains, aromas characteristic for a certain degree of roasting of grains;
– knowledge and ability to assess the tastes;
– the ability to cook up to 40 types of coffee (cappuccino, latte, ristretto and others);
– be able to balance during the day grinding, water temperature, pressure in the coffee machine, the amount of coffee per cup, the strength of ramming and the time of passage

of water;
- the ability to draw on coffee foam (latte art).

Lounge staff
The supervisor of the lobby bar, the barman and the waiters belong to it.
Duties:
– greeting and customer service in Lobby bar;
– preparation of the hall, table setting;
– opening and closing shift;
– preparation and release of drinks in the bar;
– maintaining the cleanliness of the workplace during the shift;
– maintaining a high level of service that meets corporate standards;
– reporting.

3.6.2. Kitchen

In the kitchen of a good hotel restaurant there is a large set of staff. Cooking can be organized separately for each type of food. In this case we are talking about the brigade system of work (Partie system). This structure is only in high-class large restaurants. In restaurants smaller and simpler, the same person can perform several duties.
The type of organization of the kitchen depends on:
– restaurant menu;
– type of restaurant;
– the size of the restaurant by the number of visitors and by the volume of food services;
– physical parameters, equipment.

Chef (Executive chef, Head chef, Chef de Cuisine)
He leads the kitchen. His duties include:
– drawing up applications for the necessary food products, semi-manufactures and raw materials;
– ensuring timely receipt from the warehouse, monitoring the timing, assortment, the quantity and quality of their receipt and sale;

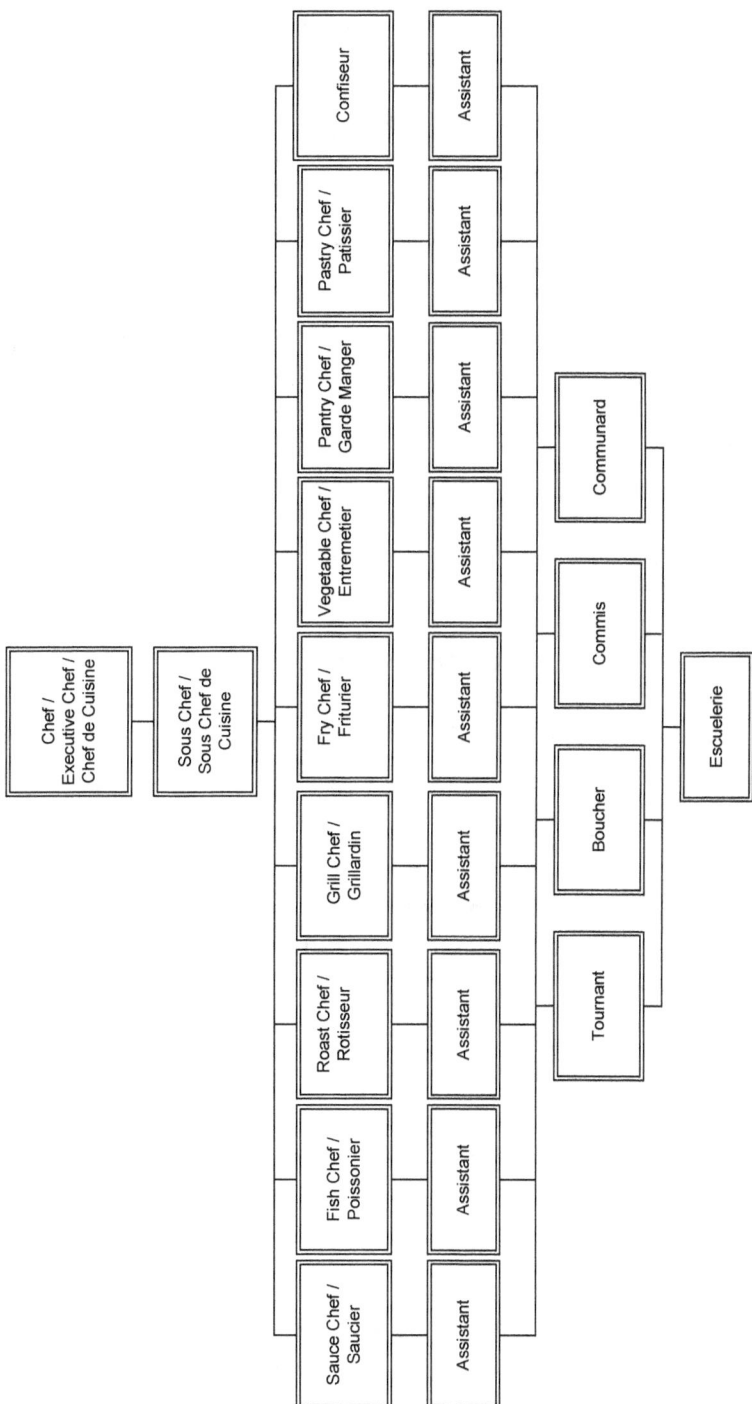

Figure 14. Hotel kitchen organizational structure

– providing, on the basis of consumer demand studies, a variety of assortment of dishes and culinary products, compiling a menu;

– control over the technology of cooking, the rules of laying raw materials and compliance with workers' health requirements and personal hygiene rules;

– arrangement of cooks and other production staff;

– scheduling of cooks;

– control of meal preparation and its readyness;

– accounting, compiling and timely reporting on production activities, the introduction of advanced techniques and methods of work;

– training.

Sous-chef

In translation means «under the chef». Assistant and Deputy Chef. Responsible for:

– preparation of products;

– coordination and preparation of the menu;

– general supervision of the kitchen;

– acceptance of orders and a command for the beginning of preparation;

– schedule of work;

– internal logistics;

– is able to replace the chef, if necessary.

He can also help the rest of the cooks. In large industries, there can be several positions of sous-chef.

Cook (Chef de Partie, Chef de parti)

Actually, the cook. Responsible for a certain direction of culinary production. If the production is large, the chefs de party can have assistants and deputies. Most of the chef de party on each type of production is just one, for a larger structure, it is customary to refer to «the first cook», the «second cook»" and so on. They differ in the directions:

Sauté Chef, Saucier (sautées, sauce) – responsible for sauces, for everything served with sauce, also for stewing and roasting in sauces. Requires the highest preparation and responsibility.

Fish Chef, Poissonier (fish cook, poissonne) – prepares fish dishes, can be responsible for cutting fish and for specific fish sauces/gravies.

Roast Chef, Rotisseur (meat cook, rotisser) – prepares meat dishes, and their sauces. Cutting meat is not engaged. Often rotisserie also performs the work of grilliarde.

Grill Chef, Grillardin (grilled chef, grilliardien, sometimes grilled) – responsible for cooking dishes on the grill, also on an open fire.

Fry Chef, Friturier (cook-roasting, deep fryer) – a separate position of the person involved in roasting food components (more often meat, so combined with rotissie). He is also a fryer bath operator (usually with an assistant).

Vegetable Chef, Entremetier (entremete) – prepares salads and first courses, as well as vegetable garnishes and vegetable decorations. When a large load is divided into:

– Soup Chef, Potager (the chef of the first dishes, potayte);

– Vegetable dishes cook, Legumier (chef of vegetable dishes).

Pantry Chef, Garde Manger – responsible for cold snacks – and usually for all meals that are prepared and served cold. If necessary, and for salads.

Pastry Chef, Pâtissier (cook bakery, pattissier) – is responsible for baking, baked dishes.

Confectioner – responsible for desserts.

Secondary posts

Roundsman, Tournant (replacement chef) is a chef whose task is to be an assistant to a chef de parti at the right time.

Butcher, Boucher – is responsible for the primary cutting of meat (game, poultry) and fish, also, if necessary – for subsequent cutting.

Apprentice, commis is the name of the chef, who understands the essence of the work of the kitchen department, or the chef who changed the department.

Communard (domestic chef, «home cook») – prepares dishes for the hotel's staff, including for the kitchen chefs.

Dishwasher, escuelerie (esculer, esculier) – one or more people washing dishes during work, as well as keeping a clean and sanitized kitchen. Dishwashers may be divided by the types of dishes (glass, appliances, etc.).

In general, the functioning of the hotel restaurant is somewhat different from the work of an ordinary restaurant. The operating time of the hotel restaurant should be such as to satisfy the vast majority of guests, even if in some hours the work of this restaurant will not bring profit. At the same time, up to 70% of hotel guests do not have dinner in the hotel restaurant and up to 50% do not have dinner in it, and 2/3 of the restaurant revenue comes from third-party visitors. Accordingly, the hotel restaurant should have a separate entrance from the street and its autostation.

Until the 1950's the restaurant in the hotel was a secondary source of income. Sometimes he was even a burden to the owner of the hotel. It was assumed that a small loss-making capacity of the restaurant was allowed, which was covered by income from a no-dimensional fund.

As the number of hotels decreased, the role of the food service as a source of income began to increase. Hotel restaurants are becoming more luxurious, the number of them in one hotel is increasing, there are specialized restaurants with national cuisines, coffee shops, bars, etc. Now the higher the class of the hotel, the more significant is the role of the restaurant.

Usually the GM of the hotel is not very well versed in the restaurant business. Therefore, quite often the hotel restaurant with all equipment is rented to a professional restaurateur.

Management of public catering in the hotel quite independently, for example, the advertising campaign of the restaurant is held separately from the hotel advertisement.

If the restaurant purchases the goods itself, then may be also such staff as a food purchaser and a purchaser of wines and other beverages.

If there are several restaurants in the hotel, then everyone has a director and an individual director at the Room Service, which delivers food and drinks to the hotel rooms.

If there are several restaurants in the hotel, then each of them should have an even image, while the interior of each should match the menu and the client.

In addition to restaurants, a large hotel necessarily has several smaller catering enterprises: bars, coffee shops, buffets, etc.

3.7. Security department

The hotel is a place of rest and, as a result, an increased concentration of people. The hotel administration assumes the responsibility not only to ensure a cozy stay and guarantees a good rest, but also a guarantee of the safety of people. That is why, careful control is needed in the sphere of hotel security.

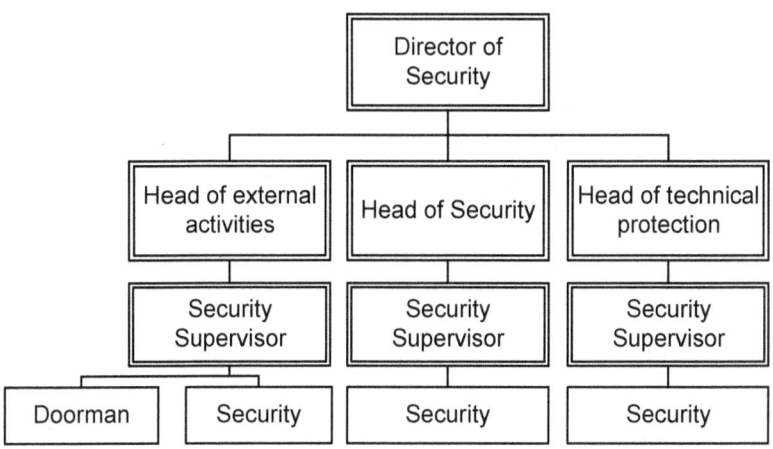

Figure 15. Hotel Security department organizational structure

The hotel security system is complex, multi-level and multi-functional. The effective hotel security system includes:
– organization of measures to ensure the safety of guests and their property;
– protection of hotel property;
– ensuring the safety of hotel staff;
– ensuring the business security of the hotel business.
Besides:
– accounting, storage, operation and cancellation of equipment and property belonging to the hotel itself;
– timely and effective control over the financial and business and commercial activities of the hotel (accounting, business agreements, taxes, leases, etc.);
– legal security of the hotel, providing for timely registration and legitimacy of all types of activities, licensing and certification of the services provided;

– timely registration and introduction in the company's statutes and collective agreements of additions related to changes in the forms of ownership of hotel, the rights and duties of their owners;

– reflection in the job descriptions and in other documents (in memos, regulations, acceptance and transfer acts, etc.) of direct duties and personal responsibility of hotel employees to ensure security in the sites of their work.

The hotel security service deals with the following problems:

– providing access control for guests and staff;

– protection of buildings and premises;

– protection of equipment and territory;

– control over the movement of material values;

– maintenance of the order in places of possible congestion of visitors;

– protection of life and health of employees and guests;

– protection of property of guests, including those deposited in the hotel's luggage storage room;

– search for lost property of guests and employees;

– advising on security issues;

– organization of evacuation of guests and personnel in emergency situations;

– implementation of a set of preventive measures to prevent violations of the law on the territory of the hotel;

– drawing up a list of information relating to commercial secrets;

– evaluation of documents from the point of view of inclusion in them of excessive data;

– drawing up a list of persons admitted to trade secrets;

– taking measures to store, copy, use commercial information in the destruction of media;

– taking measures that preclude the disclosure of trade secrets;

– preparation of an information dossier on the risk group's employees (leading experts and persons admitted to trade secrets);

– verification of information about persons who are going to work in a hotel;

– organization of work to upgrade the skills of security officers;

– design and installation, maintenance of security and fire alarm systems;

– development of employee action plans in emergency situations, evacuation schemes, installation of signal indicators;

– training of fire safety officers;

– conducting training activities on actions in emergency situations;

- conducting competitive intelligence activities;

– market research, information gathering for negotiations;

– establishment of trustworthiness of business partners;

– establishing the circumstances of the misuse of brand names, patented technologies and other information relating to the intellectual property of the hotel.

Security personnel are limited in rights compared to police: they do not have the right to interrogate, search and conduct other actions, so the main task of the security service is not to investigate committed crimes, but to prevent them.

At the head of the security service is the chief, who is managing the departments of the guards, the engineering protection team, the security team of external activities.

For the successful operation of the security service, it is very important to have a good relationship with other parts of the hotel, primarily with the financial department and the personnel department.

The security department should have a good relationship with the local police department, from which it can receive useful information about the possible appearance of unwanted guests, anticipated demonstrations, riots and other events that could disrupt the hotel's calm operation. At the same time, this cooperation should not go too far: one should not transfer to law enforcement bodies any information about the guests of the hotel, except in cases stipulated by law. It is also not advisable to provide these facilities with a hotel room for special operations, which could damage the reputation of the hotel.

The security department is developing a project of the hotel security system, which is approved by the GM after discussion with the heads of other divisions. This document covers all aspects of security (the functions of the security, its relationship with other units, the system of technical security equipment, the operation of hotel employees in critical situations – fire, explosion threat, etc.).

Sometimes security department is managing doormen and pages.

Employees of the security service when entering a job are necessarily trained, during which they are introduced in detail to the hotel, its units, typical situations, rights and responsibilities, methods of providing first aid, and how to write an investigation report. Security officers, of course, should be well aware of all laws relevant to their work and hotel activities.

To the senior management of the hotel security service periodically provides a report with the analysis of incidents (the most frequent incidents, where they most often occur, at what time, which names are associated with these incidents), which suggests measures to eliminate the recurrence of such incidents. Security departmnent should records all incidents, complaints and results of investigations.

3.8. Human resource department

Functions of the Human resource (HR) department of the hotel are related to:

− selection, recruitment, assessment of the quality personnel, training the hotel staff;

− conflict resolution, formation of corporate consciousness;

− development of job descriptions and functional technologies for personnel;

− assessment and assistance in improving the working conditions of workers;

− help the heads of the hotel departments in the work with the person;

− staff development;

− encouraging and motivating staff and so on.

HR manager

The structure of the HR in hotel depends on its size. The head of the service is a manager who is managing several managers who are responsible for certain areas of work.

HR manager is responsible for:

− short-term and long-term planning of the department's activities;

– coordination of work with other departments;

– tracking the implementation of corporate standards;

– organization of a policy of «openness» for staff, its requests, complaints, proposals, etc.;

– providing information on HR policy, legal requirements, arbitration;

– ensuring the needs of the hotel in personnel, assistance to managers in the whole process of recruiting;

– providing standards for storage and processing of personal data of employees;

– providing information on incentives / penalties / behavior of staff;

– analysis of employee turnover, development of retention policy, interviewing of outgoing employees;

– training of the employees of the department;

– reporting.

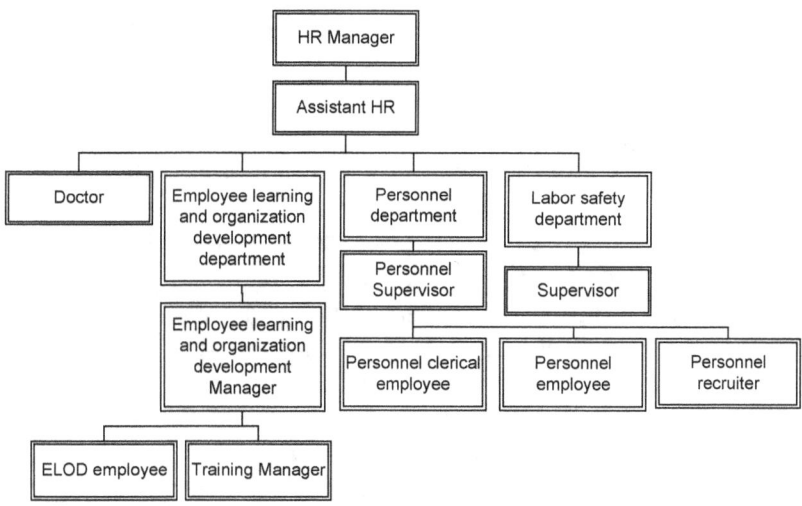

Figure 16. Hotel Human resources department organizational structure

Manager of Employee Learning and Organization Development (ELOD)

Main responsibilities:

– to carry corporate values and philosophy;

– ensure the strategic integrity of training and development in

accordance with the mission and vision of the hotel;
– determination of the needs for the development of hotel staff;
– provision of the necessary training of personnel;
– monitoring the effectiveness of training and development activities;
– coordination of training programs;
– promotion and informing of personnel about existing programs;
– making changes and adjustments to the training methodology;
– providing additional training;
– organization of a program for the development of top management;
– training of employees of the department;
– development of a training calendar;
– tracking the introduction of learning outcomes into practice;
– tracking of key indicators (employee and guest satisfaction, financial results).

Training manager
In close cooperation with the ELOD manager he is responsible for:
– informing the departments about the need for training;
– providing with necessary trainings;
– leadership of the trainers of departments;
– evaluation of trainings for departments;
– reporting on the training conducted;
– management of own employees;
– searching and organization of trainings, training companies
– management of the cross-training program;
– preparation of quarterly training plans;
– ensuring the work of innovation programs;
– making press releases on programs and learning outcomes;
– participation in team building programs;
– introductory training for new employees (orientation training).

Personnel department includes a supervisor and ordinary employees, whose duties include:

– recruitment of employees;
– assessment of available labor resources;
– assessment of future needs;
– management of personal affairs of hotel employees;
– attestation of personnel;
– evaluation of the results of work activity (determination of conscientiousness of performance of duties, degree of labor efficiency, identification of the most promising employees, definition of criteria for promotion, dismissal, etc.);
– development and implementation of a motivation system (bonuses, paid leaves, sick leave, salary increase, birthday gifts, birth of children, anniversary of work in the department, retirement, annual staff holidays, etc.);

Labor Safety department is responsoble for:
– organization and coordination of work on labor protection in the enterprise;
– control over the compliance in the structural units of legislative and regulatory legal acts on labor protection;
– carrying out preventive work to prevent industrial injuries, occupational and production-related diseases;
– conducting activities to create healthy and safe working conditions at the enterprise, for providing employees with established benefits and compensation for working conditions;
– attestation and certification of workplaces and production equipment in accordance with the requirements of labor protection;
– consideration of accidents and development of measures for their prevention;
– preparation of documents for payment of compensation for harm caused by the health of workers as a result of an accident at work or occupational disease;
– organization of inspections of the technical condition of buildings, structures, equipment, machinery and mechanisms for compliance with their requirements of regulatory legal acts on labor protection, the state of sanitary facilities;
– development of the «Labor Protection» section of the collective agreement;
– providing introductory and repeated briefings, training and testing of knowledge on labor protection of employees of the

enterprise;

– consideration of letters, applications and complaints of employees on labor protection issues.

Doctor
Duties:
– providing staff with a permanent, emergency and urgent first medical aid;
– planning and analysis;
– organization and independent conduct of special diagnostic studies;
– registration of medical documentation;
– examination of incapacity for work of employees;
– checking, tracing the medical records of each employee (health records);
– equipment of a medical center: ordering of medicines, vitamins and dressing materials;
– a primary inspection of guests on their complaints, the call of specialized ambulance;
– control of the sanitary condition of the hotel, adjacent territory, catering enterprises;
– reporting.

3.9. Financial department

The financial department of the hotel is headed by the financial director (controller, chief accountant).

In hotels, the financial department may include different departments, for example:
– accounting Department;
– financial department;
– tax policy department;
– procurement department;
– cost control department.

The financial department provides financial data used by all managers in the daily decision-making process, which ensures the financial well-being and prosperity of the hotel.

The department is engaged in raising the financial literacy of the management, providing recommendations on desirable economic options, protecting assets of owners through reliable internal control systems, and preparing forecasts and preparing monthly and annual reports.

Employees of the department should have excellent analytical skills, a mathematical mindset, able to cope with numerous tasks and work independently.

3.9.1. Accounting department

Accounting department is responsible for maintaining records for all transactions. At the end of each month and year provides information on all assets, losses of the state. If there are discrepancies, it checks and corrects. Carries out calculations of wages and other charges.

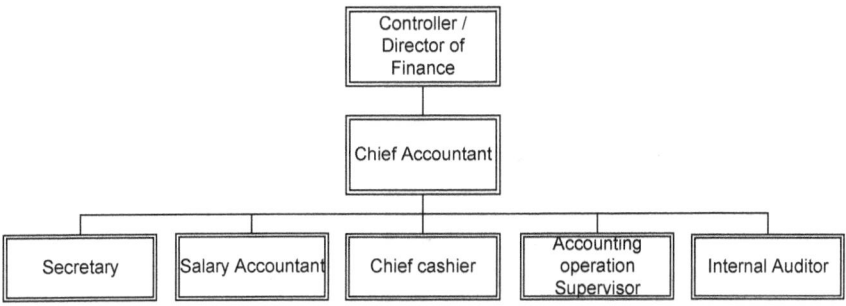

Figure 17. Hotel Accounting department organizational structure

Key responsibilities:
– control of all transactions;
– reporting on accounts and comparison with forecasting indicators;
– preparation of profit and loss statements;
– assistance in budgeting of hotel departments;
– reconciliation of bank statements;
– tracking of legislation;
– tracking of payment delays;
– tracking of unreliable debtors;
– monitoring of cash flow.

The work of the secretary, accountants in different areas is understandable. Consider the Chief Cashier and the Internal auditor.

Chief cashier:
– carries out operations on receipt, accounting, issuance and storage of cash and securities with mandatory observance of the rules ensuring their safety;
– receives cash and securities in banks;
– conducts on the basis of income and expenditure documents cash book, reduces the actual availability of cash and securities with a book balance;
– draws up cash accounts;
– takes money from the cashiers at the end of their working shift (if necessary, and in other cases);
– ensures the uninterrupted operation of the cash registers of the enterprise, monitors the absence of violations of the rules of trade in the work of the cash offices.

Internal Auditor:
– check of accounting and documentation
– revealing facts of violation of the reflection of business transactions on the accounts of accounting;
– verification of compliance with the procedure for accounting and reporting to the requirements of the legislation;
– control compliance with the requirements for the processing of primary documents;
– rendering consultations to heads of departments in the field of methodology of accounting and tax accounting;
– development of regulations, internal standards, methodologies and regulations for record keeping;
– evaluation of the work of employees of the accounting service.

3.9.2. Purchasing department

The main function of the department is to purchase the necessary goods of the required quality at a reasonable price at the right time. At the same time, the optimal size of the stock in the hotel should be maintained, as storage costs money, besides many goods can deteriorate.
The goods purchased for the needs of the hotel are divided

into the following main groups:
- products (fresh, frozen, canned, dried);
- beverages;
- equipment and furniture (as worn and broken), dishes, linen;
- consumables (mainly used for cleaning rooms and public premises).

When choosing suppliers, the following are considered:
- supplier reputation;
- the price of the product and its quality;
- volume of the lot;
- terms of payment;
- service of the purchased goods;
- the cost of delivery, the distance to the supplier etc.

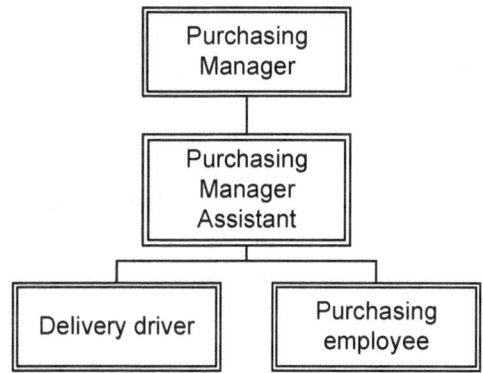

Figure 18. Hotel Purchasing department organizational structure

Purchasing department uses long-term contracts with suppliers and one-time purchases.

Long-term contracts allow you to get a discount in the price and greatly simplify the work of the department. However, this procurement method has its drawbacks. The volume of periodic supplies is fixed in the contract. Therefore, with an unexpected decline in hotel occupancy, surpluses arise, and with a sharp increase in the occupancy, there is a shortage of goods. There are cases when the quantity of the delivered goods ceases to satisfy the customer, and it is difficult to break the contract. The price of goods on the market may fall, and the hotel must pay at the price fixed in the contract.

Due to this situation, a number of purchases are made daily by different suppliers. This is done to minimize the price. Some products can even be purchased in retail. This method has a disadvantage: a certain product can simply be absent from the market at the moment.

By the wholesale the hotel buys wine, spirits, beer, tobacco and meat. If the hotel enters the hotel chain, then at least a part of the necessary goods it receives through the system of centralized purchases of this chain. This system has central warehouses, from which deliveries are made.

Purchasing is made as follows:
– all hotel services submit detailed orders to the purchasing department: the size, weight, country of delivery, quantity and date of delivery are specified;
– the purchasing department manager specializing in the declared goods, considers suppliers' offers (price, possible discounts, payment forms, etc.), chooses the best and draws up an order;
– when the goods arrive, they check, register, register the return of the unmarketable goods;
– when an invoice is received from a supplier, it is checked, registered and sent for payment to the financial service.

Head of Purchasing department
Duties of purchasing manager are:
– work with suppliers of products necessary to ensure the operation of hotels: negotiations, contractual work, lobbying the interests of the company, controlling the supply of products, control of mutual settlements;
– control of procurement prices, both for consumables, products and fixed assets;
– organization of participation in tenders;
– participation in the selection of the personnel of the department;
– supply control;
– administrative and economic activity;
– organization of the department;
– purchase of products;

– control of goods movement, drawing up of applications;
– drawing up and tracing schedules of deliveries;
– control of balances in the warehouse, goods logistics, invoices, overheads;
– coordination with other departments.

Purchasing specialist:
– ensures the availability of goods for their product groups in the optimal quantity and range;
– provides planned indicators for the turnover of its commodity groups;
– searches for suppliers, studies new proposals from suppliers, prepares for management informed proposals on attracting new suppliers;
– negotiates with suppliers and agrees terms of delivery with the direct supervisor;
– makes orders to suppliers;
– monitors the execution of the order;
– provides documentary execution of transactions;
– defines the minimum stock balance;
– provides the departments and services of the company with all necessary information about the goods.

The delivery-driver
Duties:
– ensuring the technically sound condition of the car assigned to the driver;
– taking measures to protect the car and property located in it;
– acceptance of goods from warehouses in accordance with accompanying documents;
– checking the integrity of the packages;
– control of the correctness of loading and unloading operations, placement and packing of goods in the car;
– ensuring the safety during transportation;
– registration of documents for the delivery of goods. Is a trustee of the enterprise when handing over, receiving and transporting the goods;
– development of the route, coordination of the route;
– keeping track sheets.

3.9.3. Cost control department

Cost control department is managing and reducing the costs. The task is to determine the existing costs and to assess their justification, as well as various measures to reduce. It affects all the processes of the hotel.

Typically, Cost control includes:

− study of business procedures, comparison of actual costs with budgets;

− an estimation of the reasons of occurrence of deviations;

− correction of procedures.

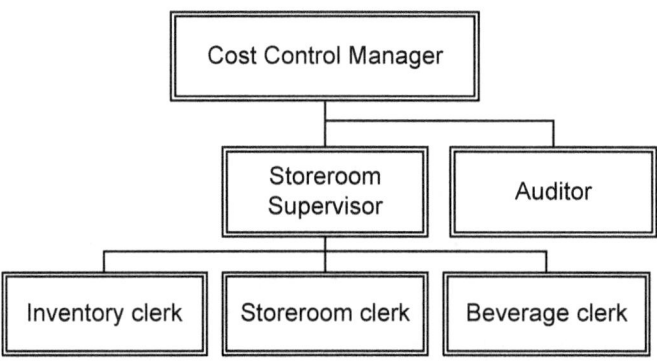

Figure 19. Hotel Cost control department organizational structure

Head of Cost Control Department:

− develops procedures for controlling costs;

− verification of accounts of supplier companies;

− registration of goods received;

− preparation of invoices for payment;

− control over the movement of goods: receipt, storage, delivery;

− participation in the inventory;

− calculation of monthly, quarterly and annual reports on food products, drinks, mini-bars, etc.;

− calculation of costs for all units;

− calculation of costs for new hotel products, menu dishes;

− analysis of the units;

− audit of suppliers' prices;

− ensuring the control over the storage of goods;

Warehouse (Storeroom) Supervisor
Duties:
– personnel control;
– solution of emerging problems with food/beverages;
– quality control of goods in the warehouse;
– control of incidental expenses;
– control of sanitary standards and conformity of hotel policy in the field of storage and procurement;
– preparation of daily and weekly orders for goods;
– inventory.

Inventory / Storeroom / Beverage clerk
Duties:
– receipt, storage, issue, security of goods/drinks in the warehouse;
– record keeping of goods/drinks;
– ensuring sanitary standards;
– inventory;
– control of the level of stocks.

3.10. Information technology (IT/EDP) department

IT department is engaged in the introduction, development and support of computer and communication systems in all divisions of the hotel.

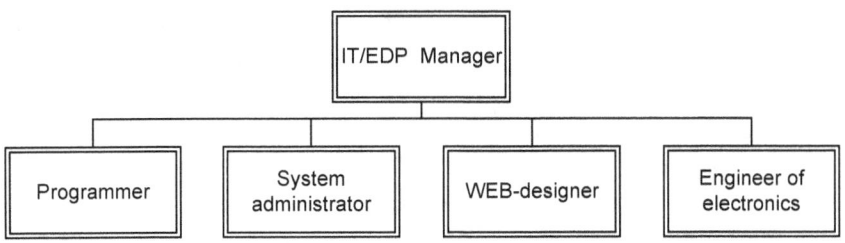

Figure 20. Hotel IT department organizational structure

In its charge: the technical support of the hotel: a set of powerful servers, automated workstations, computer networks, telephone communication systems, etc.

IT/EDP Manager:
– organization of work of the IT department in the hotel;
– planning, implementation, development and further maintenance of the hotel's IT infrastructure, including business applications, back-office, telephony, telecommunications, information security systems;
– ensuring compliance of all IT processes with company standards;
– support for users of IT systems, prompt elimination of problems and problems;
– implementation of selection, purchase, installation, use and maintenance of computer and network equipment and hotel software;
– ensuring the continuous operation of all telecommunications systems of the hotel, including phones, Internet, TV systems, etc.
– interaction with subcontractors in IT;
– management of all IT projects of the hotel, participation in related projects; conducting trainings for specialists of the department and employees of other divisions of the hotel;
– development of measures and their implementation to protect hotel information, ensure the sustainability of all IT systems of the hotel;
– budgeting for IT and telecommunications, controlling the amount of expenses for these purposes, preparing internal reports for the management of the hotel.

Programmer:
– develops programs that provide the ability to perform tasks with computer facilities, conducts their testing and debugging;
– develops a technology for solving the problem for all stages of processing information;
– determines the information to be processed by means of computer technology, its volumes, structure, layouts and schemes of input, processing, storage and output, methods of its control;
– performs work on preparing programs for debugging and debugging;
– runs debugged programs and input the initial data, determined by the conditions of the tasks;
– adjusts the developed program based on the analysis of output data;

– develops instructions for working with programs, prepares necessary technical documentation;
– provides support for the implementation of programs and software.

System Administrator:
– installs network software on servers and workstations;
– configures the system on the server;
– provides integration of software on file servers, servers of database management systems and on workstations;
– maintains the operational status of the server software and workstations;
– registers users, assigns identifiers and passwords;
– train users to work in the network, keeping archives;
– monitors the use of network resources;
– organizes access to local and global networks;
– sets limits for users;
– provides timely copying and data backup;
– is involved in restoring the system's operability in case of failures and outages of network equipment;
– monitors the network, develops proposals for the development of network infrastructure;
– provides network security (protection against unauthorized access to information, viewing or changing system files and data);
– prepares proposals for the modernization and acquisition of network equipment;
– monitors the installation of equipment by specialists of the local organizations.

Web Designer:
– creates information, commercial objects;
– exchanges information, gives recommendations when creating objects, participates in their adaptation;
– undertakes purposeful actions for obtaining all information on the location of objects on the Internet;
– directly takes part in the preparation of facilities for production, including with the involvement of outside experts, if necessary;
– carries out the author's supervision, personally decides on the start of the location of objects on the Internet;

– controls the placement of objects on the Internet;
– analyzes the experience of competitors.

Electronic engineer:
– ensures correct technical operation, uninterrupted operation of electronic equipment;
– participates in the development of prospective and current plans and work schedules, maintenance and repair of equipment, measures to improve its operation, prevent marriages and downtime, improve the quality of work, and efficient use of electronic equipment;
– provides preparation of electronic computers for work, technical inspection of individual devices and assemblies, monitors the parameters and reliability of electronic equipment elements, conducts test checks with the purpose of timely detection of faults, and eliminates them;
– performs adjustment of elements and blocks of electronic computers, radio electronic equipment and individual devices and assemblies;
– organizes technical maintenance of electronic equipment, provides an operable condition, rational use of it, carrying out preventive and routine repairs;
– exercises control over repair and testing of electronic equipment, observance of operating instructions, technical maintenance of it;
– keeps records and analyzes the indicators of the use of electronic equipment, studies the operating modes and conditions of its operation, develops regulatory materials on the operation and maintenance of electronic equipment;
– makes requests for equipment and spare parts, technical documentation for repairs, reports on the work;
– carries out control over the timely provision of electronic equipment with spare parts and materials, organizes the storage of radio electronic equipment.

3.11. Sales & Marketing department

The department is engaged in search and attraction of new clients, support of interaction with existing clients, increase in sales volume.

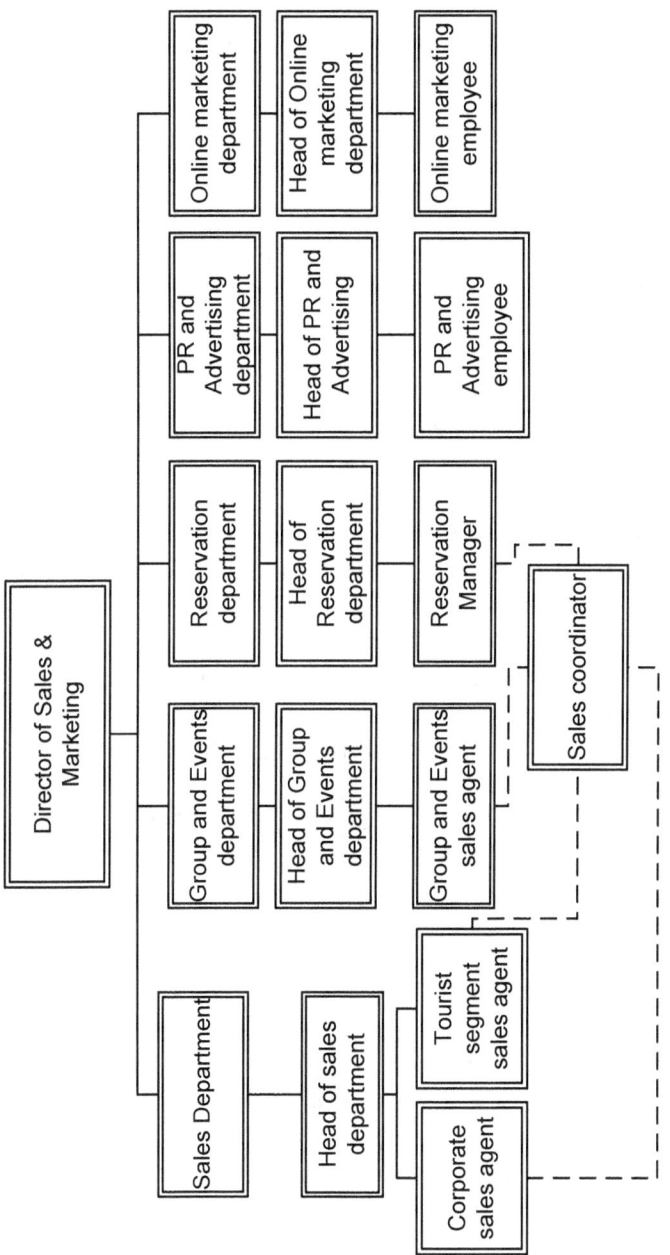

Figure 21. Hotel Sales & Marketing organizational structure

Head of S&M department is S&M Director (or S&M Manager). His duties:
– personnel management, work supervision, KPI performance monitoring, adaptation, training, professional development;
– search and attraction of new corporate clients, support of interactions with the existing customer base and further increase in sales;
– conducting presentations of services for clients, special client activities, preparation of tender documents;
– marketing and monitoring of competitors' market, appearance of new products, price offers;
– work at exhibitions;
– tracking financial relationships with customers, analytics and sales statistics, reporting work;
– development of package proposals.

Head of sales / Head of group and events sales department:
– organization of measures to attract individual clients (tourist and corporate segment) to cooperate with the hotel;
– study of hotel market in the region;
– development and organization of events for stimulating the activity of individual (corporate) clients;
– preparation of loyalty programs and various motivational short-term offers for clients;
– constant contact with companies that have contractual relations with the hotel, systematic information about new services, discounts and events;
– daily monitoring of sales in online booking systems;
– sales analysis and reporting;
– an analysis of the wishes and requests of the hotel's customers for further suggestions for improving the quality, changing and expanding the scope of rendered services;
– work with individual (group) requests at all stages;
– work with requests for events in the conference rooms;
– conclusion of contracts, work with documentation;
– promotion of the services provided by the hotel.

Sales agent:
– search for potential customers;
– conducting commercial negotiations with customers;

– processing of orders of clients, draws up necessary documents;

– finding out the customers' needs for the products sold by the hotel, and coordinating the orders with the client in accordance with its needs;

– motivation of clients to work with the hotel in accordance with approved programs to promote sales;

– preparation of a monthly sales plan;

– keeping records on sales;

– maintenance of the client base.

Head of Reservation Department:

– planning and control of the activities of the department;

– selection and management of personnel;

– segregation of duties between the reservation department's employees;

– interaction with service providers (GDS);

– ensuring the quality of customer service;

– participation in drawing up contracts with corporate clients (regarding hotel reservations).

Reservation manager (reservation agent):

– provides the client with oral and written information on the placement and sale of numbers in the client's language;

– preliminary booking of places in the hotel by phone, telex and fax;

– keeps records on reservations.

PR and advertising department

Duties of the head of department:

– organization of work in the field of communications: addressing any issues affecting public relations and affecting the image of the company;

– organization of various publications about the company, writing news and press releases and their distribution in the media, presentations and press conferences;

– organization and holding of image events, including charity;

– resolution of conflict situations, threatening the reputation of the company, responses to received complaints from consumers;

– organization of effective internal communication: holding meetings, meetings and corporate trainings, issuing a corporate newspaper, etc.;

– development of a plan for conducting PR-campaigns of the enterprise and drawing up a forecast of their influence on the image of the enterprise;

– definition of the budget of PR-campaigns;

– analysis of the effectiveness of the activities carried out;

– development of marketing policy based on analysis of consumer properties and demand forecast;

– compilation of prospective and current production plans, identification of new sales markets and new product consumers;

– coordination of all functional units for the collection and analysis of commercial and economic information, the creation of a database on marketing of enterprise products;

– organization of the study of consumers' opinion about the products produced by the enterprise, its influence on sales and preparation of proposals to increase its competitiveness and quality;

– preparation of proposals for the formation of corporate identity of the enterprise and corporate design of promotional products.

Online Marketing Department

The main object is promotion of the hotel on the Internet, hotel advertising, work with the site:

– planning and organization of the entire network interaction of the hotel;

– work in social networks;

– online marketing campaigns;

– evaluation of the effectiveness of online marketing;

– evaluation of online trends, cost optimization based on this estimate;

– generation of ideas and new creative approaches;

– cooperation with online agencies.

Sales Coordinator

The sales coordinator does everything except direct sales. His duties include:

– assistance to sales managers, coordination and support of

the sales process;
- formation of orders, invoicing;
- reporting;
- conducting business correspondence with customers.

In addition to these departments in each specific hotel there may be changes / additions related to the specifics of the enterprise.

Who else can be:
- guest relation manager (for example, as part of FO);
- swimming pool / health complex (administrator);
- laundry / dry cleaning (if own);
- etc. etc.

Questions for self-examination

1. What is organization structure of hotel?
2. What departments are included in hotel structure?
3. What are the key duties of General manager of hotel?
4. Describe Rooms division organizational structure.
5. Describe Food & Beverages organizational structure.
6. Describe Financial department organizational structure.
7. Describe Sales & Marketing organizational structure.

CONCLUSION

Hotel is a very complex enterprise. Guests are travelling. They need all the services outside of their place of permanent residence. So, any hotel should have staff that can meet the guest's requirements. That's why proper organizational structure is necessary for any hotel.

In this textbook all common hotel departments are described.

REFERENCES

1. Bystrov S.A. Organizaciya gostinichnogo dela. Uchebnoe posobie. M.: Forum, Infra-M, 2016. – 432 s.

2. Kozlov D. A. Avtomatizaciya gostinichnogo predpriyatiya. Micros Fidelio Front Office 7.0: Uchebnoe posobie. M.: Izd-vo Ros. ekon. akad., 2004.

3. Kozlov D.A. Yield management in hotels. USA, Charleston: CreateSpace, 2014.

4. Kozlov D.A. Quick guide to information systems in hotels. USA, Charleston: CreateSpace, 2016.

5. Kozlov D.A. Fidelio Front Office V7. USA, Charleston: CreateSpace, 2016.

6. Kozlov D.A. Information technologies in hotel business. USA, Charleston: CreateSpace, 2015.

7. Medlik S., Ingram H. Gostinichnyj biznes : uchebnik dlya vuzov. M., YUNITI-DANA, 2015.

8. Mirovoj opyt razvitiya industrii gostepriimstva / pod red. d.eh.n., prof. M.YU. Lajko. M.: Izd-vo GOUVPO "REA im. G.V. Plekhanova", 2008.

9. Organizaciya gostinichnogo dela / N.S. Rodionova. – SPb.: Troickij most, 2014.

10. Organizaciya gostinichnogo dela. Uchebnoe posobie / Pod red. L.I. CHernikovoj. M.: Knorus, – 2016.

11. Ovcharenko N. P., Rudenko L. L., Barashok I. V. Organizaciya gostinichnogo dela : uchebnoe posobie dlya bakalavrov. M., Dashkov i K., 2015.

12. Potapova I. I. Organizaciya obsluzhivaniya gostej v processe prozhivaniya: uchebnik dlya studentov uchrezhdenij srednego professional'nogo obrazovaniya. M., Akademiya, 2015.

13. Rutherford D.G., O'Fallon M.J. Hotel Management and operations. USA. New-Jersey. John Wiley & Sons, 2007.

14. SHkuropat S.G., Miheeva N.A., Skripova T.V., Marchenko E.E. Gostinichnoe delo. Uchebnoe posobie. SPb., Piter, 2016.

15. Timohina, T. L. Organizaciya gostinichnogo dela : uchebnik dlya prikladnogo bakalavriata / T. L. Timohina, Ros. gos. gumanit. un-t. – M.: YUrajt, 2016.

16. Ushakov R.N., Avilova N.L. Organizaciya gostinichnogo dela. Obespechenie bezopasnosti. Uchebnoe posobie. M.: Infra-M, 2017.

Textbook

KOZLOV DMITRY

HOTEL ORGANIZATIONAL STRUCTURE

CREATESPACE PUBLISHING

USA

2018

ISBN: 1984122223
ISBN-13: 978-1984122223

Paper size: In Octavo, 6"x9" (15.24x22.86)

www.ingramcontent.com/pod-product-compliance
Lightning Source LLC
Chambersburg PA
CBHW051329220526
45468CB00004B/1555